The Big Idea
of Biblical Preaching

The Big Idea
of Biblical Preaching

Connecting the Bible to People

In Honor of Haddon W. Robinson

Keith Willhite
and Scott M. Gibson,
editors

 Baker Books

A Division of Baker Book House Co
Grand Rapids, Michigan 49516

Published by Baker Books
a division of Baker Book House Company
P.O. Box 6287, Grand Rapids, MI 49516-6287

Paperback edition published 2003

Printed in the United States of America

Library of Congress Cataloging-in-Publication Data

The big idea of biblical preaching : connecting the Bible to people / Keith Willhite and
    Scott M. Gibson, editors.
        p.   cm.
    Includes bibliographical references.
    ISBN 0-8010-9066-0 (cloth)
    ISBN 0-8010-9158-6 (pbk.)
    1. Preaching. 2. Bible—Homiletical use. I. Willhite, Keith, 1958–   . II. Gibson,
    Scott M., 1957–   .
    BS534.5.B55   1999
    251—dc21   98-33548

For information about academic books, resources for Christian leaders, and all new releases available from Baker Book House, visit our web site:
                    http://www.bakerbooks.com

Contents

5

Introduction and Dedication

For over forty years, Haddon W. Robinson has taught in three North American seminaries, showing preachers how to communicate the Bible's big ideas with precision. This book is in honor of Haddon Robinson—for his numerous contributions to the field of homiletics, the fruit of which is known fully only by the men and women who sit week after week in padded pews or rowed chairs. All of us who have contributed to this book present it as a token of our sincere appreciation for what we have learned from Haddon Robinson. We count it a great privilege to call him "mentor," "colleague," and "friend."

Haddon Robinson is Harold John Ockenga Distinguished Professor of Preaching at Gordon-Conwell Theological Seminary, South Hamilton, Massachusetts. Writing in *Moody,* December 1986, Leslie R. Keylock cited a survey that asked leading evangelical professors of preaching who was the most outstanding professor in their field. The name mentioned more than any other was that of Haddon W. Robinson.[1]

Haddon Robinson grew up in New York City's Harlem tenement district, Mousetown. Early in life, he encountered vice, viciousness, and violence. He watched many peers turn to lives of crime and suffer early deaths. Part of the reason that Robinson did not fall into the moral cesspool that surrounded him was his Christian home. Though his mother died while he was a young boy, Robinson's memories of his father are positive. He was "a righteous man."[2] Yet his father's work required that he be gone from the home for long hours and young Haddon soon found himself a "latchkey kid."

During Robinson's early teen years, a dedicated Sunday school teacher in a Presbyterian church also deeply influenced him. John Mygatt was one of those special people who taught a class of young adolescents and loved it. Robinson observes, "I've come closer to being bored out of the Christian faith than reasoned out of it. What was so special about John Mygatt was that he prepared interesting Sunday school lessons."[3]

Though he cannot remember the exact date of his conversion, Robinson recalls that at some point in his early teen years he crossed the line from unbelief to faith. Shortly after, Dr. Harry Ironside visited the city. Young Robinson wrote in his diary: "He preached for an hour and it seemed like 20 minutes; others preach for 20 minutes and it seems like an hour. I wonder what the difference is." Finding the answer to that question became Robinson's lifelong quest. When only sixteen, Haddon Robinson left New York for Bob Jones University in Greenville, South Carolina. He often spent Friday evenings in the library reading a book of sermons and volumes on homiletics. As he listened to leading preachers in chapel, he concluded that he would become a preacher. Before graduating, he had won the Outstanding Preacher Award for a sermon on John 3:16. Next, Haddon Robinson became a student at Dallas Theological Seminary. Before going to Texas, however, he married Bonnie Vick, his college sweetheart.

In the early 1950s, homiletics was nearly unheard of at Dallas Seminary. During Robinson's senior year, some of his classmates asked him to teach an informal class in speech and preaching. Robinson comments, "I have no idea what they got out of those sessions, but it was a learning experience for me, at least!"

Haddon Robinson graduated from Dallas Seminary in 1955, planning to become an evangelist. By this time, however, his family had grown to include a daughter, Vicki. So, when the invitation came to be assistant pastor of First Baptist Church in Medford, Oregon, he accepted. He remained in Oregon only a short time, however. In 1958, Dallas Seminary asked him to return to the seminary to teach homiletics. By this time, he had dedicated his life to the teaching of preaching. He taught at Dallas Seminary for nineteen years, spending many of them as chairman of the Department of Pastoral Ministries. His new teaching ministry required additional education. By 1960, he had earned a master of arts degree in sociology and speech from Southern Methodist University. That fall, he became an instructor of speech at the University of Illinois while working on his Ph.D. in communication, which he received in 1964.

In 1979, Haddon Robinson became president of Denver Conservative Baptist Seminary. His strong desire to teach preaching persevered and so Robinson also taught homiletics at Denver Seminary, integrating exegesis courses with communication and preaching. As students learned how to exegete the Bible in interpretation courses, they continued the process through to preparing a sermon. New courses emphasized how to preach from various parts of the Bible and how to apply what is taught to life. As both professor and president, Robinson was committed to teaching future church leaders to become relevant, biblical preachers.

In 1980, Baker Book House published *Biblical Preaching: The Development and Delivery of Expository Messages* by Haddon W. Robinson. For eighteen years, numerous seminaries and Bible colleges have used the book as their primary preaching textbook. In 1991, Haddon Robinson resigned the presidency of Denver Seminary to assume the Harold John Ockenga Distinguished Professorship of Preaching at Gordon-Conwell Theological Seminary. Through preaching, leading, teaching, and writing, Haddon Robinson has led the field of evangelial homiletics. The editors and contributors of this book are pleased to dedicate this book to Haddon W. Robinson, and we do so with thanks to God for his ministry and life.

Part 1

Big Idea Preaching

Why a Single Idea Lands the Best Punch

A Bullet versus Buckshot: What Makes the Big Idea Work?

Keith Willhite

"A sermon should be a bullet and not buckshot," wrote Haddon Robinson in *Biblical Preaching*.[1] At least since Haddon Robinson's *Biblical Preaching* was published in 1980, many expository preachers and homileticians have advanced the claim that developing a single sermon idea, proposition, or thesis is the best way to preach an expository message. I write from this vantage as I am convinced of this claim, and more important, I am convinced that preaching with a single proposition is the best way to learn to preach. Having stated this claim in the classroom, less astute human beings (critically thinking students!) have asked, "Why?" I am grateful for their question, for it has sharpened my thinking and teaching. As I have discussed the question with master's and doctoral students and researched its answer, it appears that the reply consolidates under two major strands of evidence. Figure 1 provides the big picture of the argument of this chapter, which, in turn, provides the premise for this book.

Claim:	Developing a single idea in a sermon is the best way to preach, or, at least, to learn to preach.
(Why?) Evidence:	Developing a single idea or proposition in a sermon grows from evangelical hermeneutical commitments.
Evidence:	Developing a single idea or proposition in a sermon grows from a long-accepted body of rhetorical theory and practice.

Figure 1

I do not mean to suggest, of course, that all evangelicals think identically about biblical hermeneutics.[2] Nevertheless, from the essential hermeneutical commitments that we share grows the practice of propositional expository preaching.

The essential hermeneutical commitments are as follows: (1) We embrace a high view of Scripture for preaching. (2) The only way to say "thus saith the Lord" is to say what the Bible says. (3) Expository preaching requires an exegetical or hermeneutical process that requires both analysis and synthesis of the text. (4) Expository preaching is text-centered and audience-focused. Definition of these commitments as I am using them with explanation of why they generate propositional expository preaching follows.

Evangelical Hermeneutical Commitments

I have chosen the term "commitments" rather than "assumptions" for two reasons. First, I intend to argue for these commitments rather than assume them. Second, "commitment" seems to reflect the degree of embrace that biblical preachers must grant to these matters. The difference between an assumption and a commitment is like the difference between hugging Aunt Harriet and hugging the woman who just consented to become your wife. Thus, lest we assume too much, I shall delineate these commitments, even the most rudimentary, our view of Scripture.

A High View of Scripture for Preaching

Evangelicals embrace a high view of Scripture, meaning that we believe that the Bible is God's Word and it therefore has eternal authority and relevance. It speaks with authority to all people in every age and in every culture. Of course, God chose to record his Word through the events and circumstances of human history. The need for interpretation emerges in the thicket of "human history with eternal relevance."[3] Hence, as evangelicals, we do not believe that the task of interpretation is limited to historical inquiry. Likewise, we cannot interpret the eternal apart from the historical. In this thicket resides the authority that is the common denominator for those who embrace a high view of Scripture. "We affirm the complete truthfulness and the full and final authority of the Old and New Testament Scriptures as the Word of God written. The appropriate response to it is humble assent and obedience."[4] Following Osborne,[5] I prefer a carefully nuanced form of inerrancy[6] rather than the more dynamic model of Achtemeier,[7] who includes meanings added by later communities and the canonical finalization as inspired. The purpose of this brief description is not to debate the nuances or the parameters of these definitions, but to establish the commitment to the biblical text as the Word of God. As a firm affirmation of evangelical theology, David Wells has written a brief but strong appeal for biblical authority, as well as an explanation of the issues related to the range of views on authority as it relates to Scripture.[8]

For preaching, this commitment means that we accept what God's Word says as what God says. We believe, as the Bible claims, that "All Scripture is God-breathed and is useful for teaching, rebuking, correcting and training in righteousness, so that the man [or woman] of God may be thoroughly equipped for every good work" (2 Tim. 3:16–17, NIV). By implication, then, biblical preaching is profitable for teaching, rebuking, correcting, and training in righteousness. Though Paul probably wrote with the Old Testament in view, by application, we believe that all the Bible is valuable for producing good works in us. This does not mean that all of the Bible is equally valuable or that all of the Bible is of equal value for the same purposes, or equally valuable for all times and in all situations. We do affirm, however, that authority for preaching rests in the Bible. This will become all the more relevant as we look to our second hermeneutical commitment.

Say What the Bible Says

If we embrace a high view of Scripture for preaching, then surely we want to represent the Bible accurately. Closely related is the evangelical commitment that the only way to say "thus saith the Lord" is to say what the Bible says. No other preaching is genuinely biblical. As an advocate of propositional, or big idea, preaching, I do not believe that there is a single mold into which all sermons must be poured. Propositional preaching is much more a philosophy of preaching than a cookie-cutter method based on structural allegiance. Expository sermons come in many shapes and forms, but only exposition is biblical preaching at its philosophical core. At the philosophical core of "exposition" is some degree of explanation. As Haddon Robinson argued in *Biblical Preaching,* "Ideally each sermon is the explanation, interpretation, or application of a single dominant idea supported by other ideas, all drawn from one passage or several passages of Scripture."[9] Likewise, a passage, or group of passages, may have several dominant ideas from which the preacher can choose. All of these ideas are biblical exposition when preached the way they were written to the original readers. I am not suggesting, then, that the Bible was written with the intent that there is one subject and one complement per passage. Just as the preacher must make decisions about communicating biblical ideas, the exegete or interpreter must make choices to understand how some ideas support other ideas.

Walter Liefeld clarified that "expository preaching is not some narrowly defined method of outlining the text. It is not just following a passage clause by clause. Likewise, a message can meticulously deal with details of vocabulary and grammar, and still fail to explain the intended teaching and application of the author." Nevertheless, Liefeld continues, "The essence of exposition is explanation. If I explain something, I am reasonably free to choose my own method, but I must be faithful to my subject."[10] It is precisely at this juncture that careful hermeneutics and Haddon Robinson's insistence on two diagnostic questions meet. Robinson's two diagnostic questions of the text, and later of the audience, are the genius of his entire paradigm. In teaching propositional preaching I find that once students "get a lock" on these two questions, the hermeneutical-homiletical task streamlines with textual accuracy and communicative relevance. The hermeneutical questions are: (1) What is the text talking about (subject)? (2) What is the text saying about the subject (complement)? Some may ask whether these questions work equally in all genres. The answer is that they work reliably in all biblical genres, but the exegetical-hermeneutical processes for arriving at the answers must serve the genre. One does not read a paragraph of an epistle in the same way that one reads a paragraph of a narrative to discern its subject. Homiletically, the questions become: (1) What am I talking about? (2) What am I saying about the subject?[11] The answers will not be identical because the hermeneutical questions are asked in light of the biblical audience and time. The homiletical questions are asked in light of the preacher's audience and time. The correlation between the answers must be unmistakable, however, lest the preacher say something other than what the Bible says. Yet, explanation of the text or a reiteration of the text is not sufficient to constitute preaching, as we shall see in our fourth commitment.

Text-Centered and Audience-Focused Messages

Evangelicals embrace some degree of intent, whether A/authorial intent or textual intent.[12] Timothy Warren has written a concise but valuable description of the stronghold of intent on the road from exegesis to homiletics, or from hermeneutics to homiletics.[13] Warren argues that the road from text to sermon is one that begins with exegesis of the text, then moves through theology, to eventuate in homiletics. In all three phases, he asks Robinson's two diagnostic questions: (1) What is this talking about? (2) What is it saying about the subject? In the exegetical phase, only the text is considered. The exegete must "bracket out" theology and homiletics to ensure accuracy with the A/author's or text's intent. The product of the exegetical process and answering of the two questions is the exegetical idea or proposition. The exegetical proposition uses language of the text, perhaps including the biblical writer's name and the name(s) of the original audience. The time and culture of the biblical writing are included. Moving to theology, the preacher moves to more timeless language. Now, the proposition uses language that is timeless and applicable to God's people at any time. The proposition usually is stated as a timeless principle. In the homiletic phase, the exegetical proposition and theological proposition guide the way, yet the preacher gives attention to the contemporary time and audience. Moreover, the proposition gains the sense of an imperative (either explicit or implied), and hence "preaches" with the meaning intended in the exegetical proposition with the sense of "thou shalt." Figure 2 provides a simple example of the products in each phase.

By the time the preacher reaches the homiletical phase, the message remains centered in the text, giving allegiance to the same intent that Paul had for the Ephesian believers. The message also focuses on the audience, using the strong imperatival language and speaking directly to the preacher's current listeners. Hence, to use Warren's terms, the message is "text-centered" and "audience-focused."[14] Throughout the process from exegesis to homiletics, the preacher maintains an integrity with the intent and speaks a relevant word to the contemporary listener. Big idea preaching is the product of communicative choices rather than a comprehensive statement about the nature of the text. The sermon's big idea is not the only message. It is the target message for a particular audience that represents the same major intent that the passage had for its original readers.[15] Toward

Exegetical idea:	The reason Paul commanded the Ephesian believers to praise God was because God has guaranteed their future inheritance through the ministry of the Holy Spirit.
Theological idea:	Praise to God is the proper response for a guaranteed inheritance.
Homiletical idea:	Praise God because of the inheritance that the Holy Spirit guarantees to you.

Figure 2

such faithfulness with the text evangelical exegetes (and preachers) have committed themselves.

Admittedly, the tools of exegesis often emphasize analysis at the expense of synthesis. Yet, surely the exegete who seeks to represent the biblical writer's or text's intent must strive for synthesis. Otherwise, the exegete is left with a long list of lexical, grammatical, syntactical, or biblical-theological data and the burning, unanswered question, "What's the point?" This drive toward synthesis may seem like common sense for any reading, but given the life-changing, God-glorifying power of the Word of God, knowing the point is paramount. Paul wrote to correct problems in the church, to affect ecclesiastical practice, to reinforce sound doctrine. How can Scripture be "useful for teaching, rebuking, correcting, and training in righteousness"[16] if we don't "get his point?" The exegete cannot be satisfied merely with buckshot. The exegete must seek the bullet. Evangelicals' hermeneutical commitments demand no less an end.

By tracing a short list of evangelical hermeneutical commitments I have argued that these commitments seek to "say what God says" by representing the text of Scripture accurately or in line with its intention for its original readers. Developing a single idea or proposition in a sermon grows from these evangelical hermeneutical commitments. Every sermon, however, requires a series of communicative choices, not the least of which focuses on the sermon's "big idea."[17]

Rhetorical Theory and Practice

There exists a remarkable consensus among those who have studied and practiced public speaking over the last twenty-five hundred years that the most effective way to structure a speech is to build it around a single significant thought. From the ancient Greek and Roman rhetoricians to the latest communication theorists, from the preaching in the Bible to the sermons heard in pulpits today, from the political oratory of democracies long past to the persuasive message of our own times, the history of public speaking and the lessons we have learned from that history unite to argue forcefully that *a speech, to be maximally effective, ought to attempt to develop more or less fully only one major proposition.*[18]

When Aristotle wrote of the *topoi,* he argued that effective rhetoric is a single line of argument that requires the participation of the audience (an enthymeme) to complete the argument. Though his intent, in listing the *topoi,* was to suggest the necessity of a relevant topic, he posited the strategy of a single propositional line of argument.[19] This now long-accepted practice of oratory is basically assumed in many modern speech texts.[20]

That oral public communication (speech, sermon, address, announcement, etc.) should have one central thesis or idea is a strategy of communication endorsed through centuries of rhetorical theory. Indeed, we cannot imagine a skilled speaker previewing the speech: "This morning, I have a few introductory observations that don't have much to do with the rest of my talk. Then, I'd like to comment on a few things in your program, perhaps highlighting some more than others. There's one funny story I want to share with you. If time permits, I'll draw out a few implications from these comments, and then conclude with a poem. If we don't get finished, we'll pick up where we stop the next time we're together." We would surely develop little interest with such an imprecise destination in view.

As we reflect on the workings of the human mind, we soon discover why communication theorists have held to the value of the single proposition. As Duane Litfin argued, the human mind craves

Figure 3

unity, order, and progress.[21] The mind of the listener searches for overall unity. What do you see in the two drawings in figure 3?

Notice how your mind reached for a unity, some wholeness out of the parts. Likewise, we find it difficult to tolerate chaos or disunity. Our propensity toward unity makes trying to have more than one point (buckshot) like having no point at all. Narration from the musical, *The Point,* captures the idea artistically:

> Oblio and his dog, Arrow, are banished to the Pointless Forest where all things are pointless. There they meet the Pointless Man, or the Pointed Man, depending on your point of view. You see, the Pointless Man had a point. In fact he had hundreds of them. But as he so quickly pointed out, "A point in every direction is the same as no point at all."[22]

Unfortunately, too many listeners, searching for unity, are left listening to the Pointless Man.

Congruent with our desire for unity is our search for order. Typically, we are not satisfied to discover which parts are related to which whole. We seek to discover orderly relationships, sequence, ideas that follow,[23] pieces of the puzzle that, when grouped as ordered, form a unified picture.[24]

Essential to our successful search for unity via order is progress. As noted earlier, every sermon should be a reasoned argument that advances a single claim. This claim gains support from warranted evidence that either leads (inductively) to the acceptance of the claim or underpins (deductively) the acceptance of the claim. Without such progress (evidence + evidence = claim or claim = evidence + evidence), the listener is left to wander aimlessly through the Pointless Forest, with no sense of destination. But through progression, one thing following another, the preacher can argue in a rhetorically reasoned fashion so as to advance the claim or "drive home" a single big idea.[25] Progress and order work hand in hand to provide unity to the message.[26]

Conclusion

In declaring that "a sermon should be a bullet and not buckshot," Haddon Robinson consistently held to his evangelical hermeneutical commitments and followed a long-accepted strategy of rhetorical theory and practice. Though a text may say many things, listeners need to hear the synthesis of what was intended. A single bullet is much more powerful than a small piece of shot or even the collective effect of many shots. A disjointed comment on words or phrases will be of little value in changing lives since propositions of God's Truth, not minutiae, move people to think and act differently.

For Further Reflection

Getting the Idea

1. What is this chapter talking about?
2. What is this chapter saying about what it's talking about?

Building on the Idea

1. How does the preacher committed to the philosophy of preaching shape the sermon based on texts that are lists or parallel commands (e.g., 1 Thess. 5:16–22)?

2. What role should the text of Scripture play in structuring the sermon?
3. How does the preacher maintain the listeners' attention if the preacher lets the "big idea" out of the bag in the sermon's introduction?

Recommended Reading

Chapell, Bryan. *Christ-Centered Preaching: Redeeming the Expository Sermon.* Grand Rapids: Baker, 1994.

Liftin, Duane. *Public Speaking: A Handbook for Christians.* 2nd ed. Grand Rapids: Baker, 1992.

O'Day, Gail R. and Thomas G. Long. *Listening to the Word: Studies in Honor of Fred B. Craddock.* Nashville: Abingdon, 1993.

Robinson, Haddon, ed. *Biblical Sermons: How Twelve Preachers Apply the Principles of Biblical Preaching.* Grand Rapids: Baker, 1989.

Toulmin, Stephen, Richard Rieke, and Allan Janik. *Introduction to Reasoning.* New York: Macmillan, 1979.

Biblical Preaching That Adapts and Contextualizes

Scott A. Wenig

Preaching is at the heart of Christianity. It always has been and probably always will be. From the beginning of Jesus' ministry to the present day, the great biblical and theological themes of the Christian faith have been proclaimed fervently by preachers. Not all preaching, however, has been useful or effective. One contemporary homiletician, with tongue-in-cheek, asserts that many of his own sermons, along with others will, on Judgment Day, be cast into the fires of Gehenna.[1] So what is it that separates potent preaching from that which is feeble? Or, to put it in more current terminology, why do some sermons impact people while others do not?

For forty years Haddon Robinson, the father of "big idea" preaching, has argued and illustrated that effective preaching must be centered in the biblical text. Yet, what has made Haddon Robinson one of America's principal pulpiteers is his equal emphasis on relevance in preaching. Getting the Bible into the sermon is only an elementary step. If preaching is to be transformational, it must address the needs, hurts, temptations, and trials of listeners.[2] In the jargon of modern missiology, the sermon must be contextualized. As Robinson himself puts it, "Sermons . . . are not addressed 'to whom it may concern'; they are delivered to men and women sitting at a certain time of day, usually on Sunday in a building with a zip code."[3] Thus, lively sermons "are more like thoughtful conversations than scholarly lectures."[4]

As one examines Haddon Robinson's approach to preaching—both in the pulpit and in the classroom—it becomes apparent that he is part of an impressive homiletical tradition. Church history reveals that effective preachers of the past have always adapted their sermons to their audience in order to make the greatest possible impact. From the early church to modern times, the most potent preachers were those who spoke from the Bible directly to the issues of their day. The content and circumstances of preaching vary widely from generation to generation but the necessity of relevance never does. This is what pastoral theologian Thomas Oden meant when he wrote, "Preaching changes and yet remains ever the same."[5] In this essay I want to illustrate that observation by surveying briefly the preaching of four outstanding leaders in the Christian tradition: John Chrysostom, Augustine of Hippo, Martin Luther, and Martin Luther King Jr.

John Chrysostom

John of Antioch, who became known as Chrysostom (the "golden-mouthed"), was the greatest preacher of the fourth century. Some have argued that he was the finest ever to ascend a pulpit. Born to a Roman army officer and a Christian mother in 347, John was given the best education possible in Syrian Antioch. Initially trained to be a lawyer, he eventually gave up the courtroom for the solitude of the monastery. After serving as a deacon in the church for five years, John was ordained presbyter and then, at the age of thirty-nine, designated Antioch's chief preacher by Archbishop Flavian.

Ominously, less than two years later in the spring of 388, a riot erupted in the city over the imposition of new taxes by the emperor Theodosius. An enraged mob of citizens rushed into the streets and tore down five gold-plated statues of the imperial family. According to Roman law, this was a crime of treason *(laesae maiestatis),* punishable by death. Dread and panic filled the city as the governor first confiscated the ring leaders' wealth, had their families thrown into the streets, and then sent them off to face torture and death. To resolve the crisis, Archbishop Flavian left his young protégé in charge of the cathedral pulpit and set off for Constantinople to plead for the emperor's mercy.

For seven days, Chrysostom remained quiet. Then, like an Old Testament prophet summoned by God, he arose to deliver to the fearful city a series of sermons known as *On The Statutes.* He wasted no time getting to the heart of the issue:

> What shall I say, or what shall I speak of? The present season is one for tears, and not for words; for lamentation, not for discourse; for prayer, not for preaching. Such is the magnitude of the deeds daringly done; so incurable is the wound, so deep the blow, even beyond the power of all treatment, and craving assistance from above.[6]

Comparing the circumstances of Antioch to those of Job, the Golden-mouthed announced that "The city is in a death-trap! Just as Job sat on his dunghill, Antioch is . . . seated in the midst of a great snare."[7] And just as the devil inflicted enormous suffering on the great patriarch, so he has now "raged against the whole city."[8] Though John and his audience knew that Job had suffered innocently and Antioch justly, the sermon could not have been more relevant.

Like any effective preacher, John led his listeners beyond their feelings to an understanding of their problem. The cause of their suffering, he cried, was greed. Imitating the rich fool of Luke 12, they had acquired riches and things but craved even more. Worse, their covetousness spilled over into vanity and pride. "Tell me," John asked, "Why do you lead about so many servants, parasites, and flatterers, with every kind of pomp? Not for necessity, but only for pride; to the end that by these you may seem more worthy of respect than other men!"[9] They had forgotten the admonition of the apostle to the rich (1 Tim. 6:17) to be humble, not high-minded. Entangled in the web of luxury and affluence, they had become indignant when the emperor raised their taxes!

Now that calamity had fallen upon them, John applied some biblical balm to their wound. Their only hope, he said, was to admit their culpability and repent. They should not claim innocence to the emperor or fail to recognize their sin.

> [I]t is not sufficient for us to say in defense, 'I was not present; I was not an accomplice, not a participant in these acts.' 'For this reason,' he may reply, 'you shall be punished, and pay the extreme penalty, because you were not present; and did not check or restrain the rioters . . . You did not prohibit these things from being done. This is the cause of the accusation!'[10]

Anything less than complete repentance would be worthless. Only Heaven could save them now. But, if they would sincerely turn from their sin, God would honor their confession and perhaps move the emperor to relent.

For over three weeks Chrysostom preached and the people prayed. Despite the fact that the prisons filled and the executions continued, an air of hopeful calm began to pervade the city. Eventually, welcome news came from Constantinople: Archbishop Flavian had persuaded the emperor to end the punishment of Antioch. John's words proved more than relevant; they were golden!

When the good news of the pardon arrived, Chrysostom spoke aptly, as he habitually did, from the Scriptures directly to the situation. "Today," he said, "I shall begin with the same words I spoke in the time of danger. So say with me: May God be praised, who enables us this day to celebrate our festival with so light and joyful a heart. May God be praised, who is able to do exceeding abundantly above all that we ask or think!"[11]

28

Augustine of Hippo

During the same years when John Chrysostom dominated the pulpit in the eastern half of the Roman Empire, Aurelius Augustine rose to prominence in the western half. Born in North Africa in the middle of the fourth century, Augustine pursued a decadent life of wine, women, and song throughout his teens and twenties. Trained as a professor of rhetoric, he eventually moved north across the Mediterranean to Milan, but found little joy in his prestigious discipline, even calling his university appointment a "chair of lies." Unable to obtain either peace or satisfaction, he happened to encounter the saintly Ambrose, bishop of Milan, and soon thereafter experienced a dramatic conversion at age thirty-two. Less than ten years later, Augustine himself was made bishop of Hippo in his native North Africa and served there until his death in A.D. 430. Of all the Christians who have ever lived, wrote, and preached, none, with perhaps the exception of Martin Luther, has had a more profound impact on the Christian faith than Augustine.

While later generations of believers know Augustine only through his voluminous writings, the parishioners of Hippo knew him best as their preacher. During his sermons he remained seated on his throne (cathedral), usually about twelve to fifteen feet away from the congregation and always at eye level. This was intentional: he was trying to establish a degree of intimacy with his flock. And his strategy worked! On at least one occasion when he preached beyond the dinner hour, he could hear stomachs growl and rumble. Quickly, he concluded the message, saying, "Go, my very dear brothers and sisters, go and restore your strength. . . . Go then and restore your bodies so that they may do their work well, and when they are restored, come back here and take your spiritual food."[12]

Having been trained in the art of rhetoric, Augustine knew well all the strategies of communication. Yet what made him such an outstanding preacher was his emphasis on communicating God's truth in familiar and ordinary ways. The aim of the sermon, he stressed, should be to instruct, to please, and to move

29

the will to action.[13] This necessitated, above all else, being clear. To promote clarity, Augustine frequently employed illustrations, word pictures, and figures of speech common to his audience and their experience. On numerous occasions he pictured the glorious changing colors of the Mediterranean and of the creatures it held, all of which pointed to God.[14] Like any effective midwestern pastor preaching Christ in rural America, he regularly referred to his homeland, the North African countryside:

> When all is said and done, is there any more marvelous sight, an occasion when human reason is nearer to some sort of converse with the nature of things, than the sowing of seeds, the planting of cuttings, the transplanting of shrubs, the grafting of slips? It is as though you could question the vital force in each root and bud on what it can do, and what it cannot and why.[15]

As a staunch biblicist Augustine was fervently committed to preaching the Bible and its great themes, or as we might say for the purposes of this writing, its big ideas! But as all preachers know, theological concepts can be difficult to communicate. Augustine was not exempt from this challenge, but what helped make him a homiletical genius was the way he turned abstract theology into concrete images for his listeners. For example, in a sermon about God's refusal to answer some of our prayers, Augustine argued that God's superior wisdom prohibits him from doing what we, in our ignorance, sometimes ask. Then, contextualizing the concept for his audience, he spoke of a tiny child seeking to ride a huge horse: "Put me up on your horse," asks the child. "Folly," says the Father, "he would only crush you."[16] Another rather famous example comes in a sermon comparing God's gifts to a man giving his lover a bracelet:

> If she so delights in the bracelet as to forget the giver, that is an insult to him, but if she so delights in the bracelet as to love the giver more, that was what the bracelet was for. . . . We take for granted the slow miracle whereby water in the irrigation of a vineyard becomes wine. It is only when Christ turns the water into wine, in quick motion, as it were, that we stand amazed.[17]

Finally, in a sermon on the yoke of Christ (Matt. 11:28–30), Augustine used a bird and its wings to communicate that Jesus' burden was, as he said, "light":

> Now every bird carries its own wings. Watch a bird, then, and note how it folds its wings when it lights on the ground, how its wings then rest and the bird lays them along its sides. Now do you imagine the bird is burdened by them? Let it lay aside its burden and it promptly falls; the less that bird bears its burden the less is it able to fly. Would you, out of compassion, remove that burden? No, if you want to show it compassion you will leave it alone.[18]

Like Christ, Augustine had superlative skills in adapting theology to the knowledge of his audience. No wonder he was so popular with the people! It comes as no surprise, then, that one of his earliest biographers, Possidius, said, "I . . . think that men profited . . . by seeing him actually present, witnessing especially his life amongst us and hearing him preaching in the church."[19]

Martin Luther

Martin Luther needs no introduction. He personifies an era as well as a movement. He stands for the sixteenth-century Protestant Reformation and has profoundly influenced the modern world spiritually, socially, and nationally. Reformer, scholar, teacher, pastor, husband, father, composer, prayer warrior—all these labels depict Martin Luther.

Yet Luther was also a preacher—and a prolific one at that. From the beginning of his ministry in 1512 to his death in 1546, he preached over four thousand sermons. Even in years when his health was bad, Luther would often preach nearly two hundred times. Generally, he averaged three sermons per week throughout his adult life, but often preached four or more. Luther was, to state it mildly, a homiletical force.

As he did on most topics, Luther held strong opinions about preaching. It was not something he always enjoyed. On one occasion he noted:

> The office of preaching is an arduous task. . . . I have often said that, if I could come down with a good conscience, I would rather be stretched upon a wheel and carry stones than preach one sermon. For anyone who is in this office will always be plagued; and therefore I have often said that the damned devil and not a good man should be a preacher. But we're stuck with it now. . . . If I had known I would not have let myself be drawn into it with twenty-four horses.[20]

Nor did Luther think that his own preaching was always effective. After a number of years pastoring in Wittenberg, he despaired of ever preaching again. From his perspective, the congregation remained lifeless, their lives godless. In typically blunt fashion, he told them, "It annoys me to keep preaching to you."[21] When that failed to arouse their attention, he went on strike and refused to preach for a while.[22] That's one way to escape the never-ending pressure of the Sunday morning message!

Yet, in spite of his misgivings and frustrations with the responsibility of preaching, Luther was a wonderful communicator. One characteristic that stands out to the contemporary reader of his sermons is his emphasis on adapting language to the audience's level of understanding. Theology is essential, but it has to be communicated in such a way that even the youngest parishioner can hear and understand. As Luther colorfully taught his students:

> I will not consider Drs. Pomeranus, Jonas and Phillip while I am preaching; for they know what I am presenting better than I do. Nor do I preach to them, but to my little Hans and Elizabeth; these I consider. He must be a harebrained gardener who wants to consider only one flower in a large garden and neglects all the others. Therefore, see to it that you preach plainly and simply and have regard for the unlearned people and do not address only one or the other.[23]

He practiced what he taught. When the Reformation gathered momentum in Wittenberg, a radical faction attempted, in Luther's view, to move too far, too fast. Ascending the pulpit, he denounced the radicals for their lack of love toward the traditionalists in their midst. Then, using language that everyone in the congregation could understand, he spoke of a mother's love for her child.

> What does a mother do to her child? First she gives it milk, then gruel, then eggs, and soft food, whereas if she turned about and gave it solid food, the child would never thrive. So we should also deal with our brother, have patience with him for a time, have patience with his weakness and help him bear it; we should also give him milk-food too, as was done with us, until he, too, grows strong and thus we do not travel heavenward alone, but bring our brethren, who are not now our friends, with us.[24]

According to Luther, good preaching is always intelligible to an audience. "A sincere preacher," he noted, "must consider the young people, the servants and the maids in the church, those who lack education. He must accommodate himself to them as a nursing mother does to her infant . . . So preachers should also act; they should be simple in their sermons."[25]

If Haddon Robinson were to restate Luther's intent, he would say, It must always be clear! And Luther was almost always clear—even to the uneducated in the congregation. In one sermon, for example, on the fourth, fifth, and sixth commandments, Luther aimed his remarks at the layfolk. Parents, he said, must show themselves parents to their children, not tyrants, rascals, or scoundrels.[26] Masters, servants, and maids should teach their children the ways of God so that he might be honored and society improved.

> Now we must devote far more care to educating the children in order that we may find people who are capable of serving a country in its secular government and the cities in spiritual government as preachers and lectors. You see what murderous harm you do to the sovereign prince and . . . [to Germany] . . . when you keep gifted boys away from study. The same applies to you, the

33

mother of a family, if you train your daughter to be your maid badly. It is a commandment which is laid upon you, not something which is merely given to you.[27]

Like many effective preachers, Luther contextualized by using illustrations. They were an indispensable means of communicating God's Word plainly to the congregation. Luther argued that illustrations facilitated spiritual growth and theological education, especially for the average listener. As he told his preaching students, "The common people are captivated more readily by comparisons and examples than by difficult and subtle disputations. They would rather see a well-drawn picture than a well-written book."[28]

Luther often used illustrations drawn from the experiences of his audience. For example, in the sermon in which he urged patience with the pace of reform, the great Reformer called for love to those who were slow to adapt to the new order. To emphasis his point, he drew a picture for them:

> The sun has two properties, light and heat. No king has power enough to bend or guide the light of the sun; it remains fixed in its place. But the heat may be turned and guided, and yet is ever about the sun. Thus faith must always remain pure and immovable in our hearts, never wavering; but love bends and turns so that our neighbor may grasp and follow it.[29]

Despite its inherent difficulties, Luther believed that preaching was to be transformational. For that to happen, it had to be relevant and biblical. His sermons reveal his focus on the theology of gospel and an understanding of the people.[30] Haddon Robinson's label for this is "effective expository preaching"!

Martin Luther King Jr.

Of all the preachers who have contextualized and adapted the gospel message to meet the needs of contemporary audiences, none in the twentieth century has done so with more impact than

Martin Luther King Jr. If a preacher is one who heralds the heart of God to men and women, then surely this African American in the Baptist tradition is one of the truly great preachers of modern times. Born and reared in a pastor's family in the South during the Great Depression, King eventually moved north to Philadelphia to attend seminary (Crozer) and then on to Boston, where he earned the Ph.D. (Boston University). In 1954 he was called to a church in Montgomery, Alabama, but quickly rose to national prominence in the Montgomery Bus Boycott of 1955.

The Bus Boycott was, in many ways, the origin of the Civil Rights Movement in America and King remained at its center until his assassination in 1968. Rooted in the nature of the gospel and biblical ethics, the Civil Rights Movement sought to end racial segregation and promote a more just society. As was true in the black church at large, preaching was the primary motivational tool for the movement and none preached with greater power or effect than Martin Luther King Jr.

His first major sermon as a civil rights leader was given in 1955 during the boycott. At the end of the message, he concluded:

> If you will protest courageously, and yet with dignity and Christian love, when the history books are written in future generations, the historians will have to pause and say, 'There lived a great people—a black people—who injected new meaning and dignity into the veins of civilization.' This is our challenge and our overwhelming responsibility.[31]

When King walked away from the pulpit, the people jumped to their feet and gave him a thunderous ovation.

As King's leadership in the Civil Rights Movement grew, he was criticized for giving up on orthodox Christianity and simply promoting the social gospel. But his preaching lay waste to that charge. In his sermon, "The Man Who Was a Fool," King rejected secular humanism and the whole concept of human progress aided by scientific advances:

> Men believed that civilization was evolving toward an earthly paradise. Herbert Spencer skillfully molded the Darwinian the-

35

ory of evolution into the heady idea of automatic progress. Men became convinced that there is a sociological law of progress which is as valid as the physical law of gravitation . . . Then came the explosion of this myth . . . Why fool ourselves about automatic progress and the ability of man to save himself? We must lift up our minds and eyes unto the hills from whence cometh our true help . . . Without dependence on God our efforts turn to ashes and our sunrises into darkest night.[32]

For King, only Christ could save men and women from themselves. Like the apostle Paul, King proclaimed in another sermon that "God freely offers to do for us what we cannot do for ourselves. Our humble and openhearted acceptance is faith. So by faith we are saved."[33]

With the gospel as his foundation, King then preached for social change. Evil would be eliminated only when men and women gave themselves to God and allowed him to work through them. Quoting Revelation 3:20 and applying it accurately, King pleaded with his listeners to open their lives more fully to Christ.[34] This was the Christian's duty individually and the church's responsibility corporately. When this happened, social transformation would follow. As King proclaimed:

Racial justice, a genuine possibility in our nation and in the world, will come neither by our frail and often misguided efforts nor by God imposing his will on wayward men, but when enough people open their lives to God and allow him to pour his triumphant, divine energy into their souls.[35]

King's most famous sermon, "I Have a Dream," was delivered from the steps of the Lincoln Memorial on August 28, 1963. While innumerable commentators have described it as one of the most famous speeches in American history, it was, in reality, a visionary sermon of the finest sort. Rooted in the biblical imagery of Isaiah 40:4–5, the message directed the listeners to a hope that transcended the present injustice of American society.

I have a dream that one day every valley shall be exalted, every hill and mountain shall be made low. The rough places will be made plain, and the crooked places will be made straight. And the glory of the Lord shall be revealed, and all flesh shall see it together.[36]

King contextualized Isaiah's vision to the needs of the day. First, as he articulated his dream of a society based on character rather than skin color, he applied the ethic implicit in the text to challenge the racism of American society. Second, by using the text to promote both Christian faith and hope, he could encourage those active in the Civil Rights Movement to continue their work of social transformation.[37] As any preacher knows, it is easy to critique the status quo but hard to change it. Martin Luther King Jr. demonstrates how an entire society can be altered when God's preachers bring biblical truths to bear on current cultural conditions.

Haddon Robinson was right: good preachers, past and present, have always concerned themselves with both the Bible and the needs of their listeners. Transformational preaching is rooted in the sacred text but contextualized to a specific audience. This is one of the lessons of the history of Christianity. It is also a lesson Haddon Robinson has consistently brought to his students and listeners for over forty years. May we all continue to hear him and apply his message to our own preaching.

For Further Reflection

Getting the Idea

1. What is this chapter talking about?
2. What is this chapter saying about what it's talking about?

Building on the Idea

1. Can you name a few contemporary preachers who contextualize their preaching well?

2. When does "contextualization" become compromise?
3. What is the biggest hindrance to preaching contexualized messages?

Recommended Reading

Duduit, Michael. "The Preaching Tradition in America." In Michael Duduit, ed., *Handbook of Contemporary Preaching*. Nashville: Broadman, 1992, pp. 37–48.

Larsen, David L. *The Company of Preachers: A History of Biblical Preaching from the Old Testament to the Modern Era*. Grand Rapids: Kregel, 1997.

Leonard, Bill J. "Preaching in Historical Perspective." In Michael Duduit, ed., *Handbook of Contemporary Preaching*. Nashville: Broadman, 1992, pp. 21–35.

Miller, Calvin. *Spirit, Word, and Story*. Grand Rapids: Baker, 1996.

Wilson, Paul Scott. *A Concise History of Preaching*. Nashville: Abingdon, 1992.

Part 2

Big Idea Preaching

Its Biblical and Theological Power

Old Testament Interpretation Issues for Big Idea Preaching

Problematic Sources, Poetics, and Preaching the Old Testament
An Exposition of Proverbs 26:1–12

Bruce Waltke

Introduction

The Problem of Source Criticism and Preaching the Big Idea

Biblical source criticism, whether it be literary criticism, form criticism, or tradition criticism, is no friend to Haddon Robinson's concept of expositing a text by developing its big idea. To be sure, the techniques involved in identifying sources enable the expositor to isolate discreetly unified smaller texts. However, it calls into question the notion that a final redactor compiled them to communicate unifying concepts in his finished composition or in all of its parts.

Literary source criticism attempts to isolate by changes of literary style and theologies the literary sources that comprise a finished composition. Within the Pentateuch, critics of this school discern at least four distinct and sometimes contradictory documents. The preacher can present the great ideas of the source documents, but not of the whole book, because according to these critics a crude redactor pieced together the sources, contradictions and all. Indeed, a preacher worth his salt should point out these contradictions. That can lead to confusing preaching.

Form criticism is most helpful in identifying sources but presents the preacher with a different problem. This approach groups texts into genres that share the same structure, motifs, moods, vocabulary, and so on. For example, in the 50 petition psalms, the psalmist addresses God, vents his complaint that God has abandoned him and the enemy is too powerful, expresses his confidence in God, and then petitions God to deliver him. The trouble is they all seem to have the same big idea. That can lead to boring preaching.

Tradition critics attempt to trace the historical development of a source from its inception to its final form in the book. This creative process entails that the majority of Old Testament texts contain multiple levels of meaning, reflecting the gradual contribution of new individuals, groups, and generations to the text as they reinterpreted the old heritage for themselves. The preacher's problems with this approach are that critics of this school do not agree on this history and that the preacher must decide the authoritative level of meaning. That can lead to uncertain preaching.

Conservative preachers dismiss a biblical criticism that breaks Scripture apart into contradictory sources and that denies the infallibility and authority of the final text. However, they must own up to the truth that many biblical books are an anthology of sources that seem to be loosely hung together without unifying concepts.

Let me cameo the problem from the Book of Proverbs, a parade example of a "loose" anthology. According to Proverbs 25:1, the "men of Hezekiah" compiled the proverbs of Solomon in chapters 25–29. However, it is alleged that sometimes they arranged them by sound, not by sense. For example, "Like a thorn bush [that grows up] in the hand of a drunkard [*shikkor*] is a proverb in the mouth of a fool" (26:9) and "like an archer who wounds at random is he who hires [*shoker*] a fool" (26:10) were apparently linked together by their topic, "a fool," and by the sound play of *shikkor* and *shoker*, not apparently by sense. The preacher who from this paronomasia abstracts a unifying comment about a fool is engaging in eisegesis, *not* exegesis.

This cameo illustrates the problem with all sorts of Old Testament literature. The historical, prophetic, hymnic, and sapiential all consist of many originally isolated sources. Can preaching based on a great idea move with integrity beyond the textual fragments isolated by source criticism to the larger compilations?

The Contribution of Poetics

Whereas source criticism bedevils preaching the big idea of disparate texts within the finished composition or the composition itself, recent research into the poetics of the Old Testament tends to validate Robinson's popularized homiletical approach. During the last quarter of the twentieth century, scholars have turned their attention to find the rules by which redactors/authors of the biblical books assembled their sources. "We must first know how a text means," in Adele Berlin's famous phrase, "before we know what it means." Whereas the old critics regard the final text as "crudely" pieced together, critics who employ poetics have come to regard it as artistic, with careful attention having been given to detail. Robert Polzin refuses to speak any longer of redactors of the biblical books but only of their authors.[1]

The new breed of biblical critics has been developing the "grammar" of poetics.[2] Their indefatigable efforts and numerous publications have shown that biblical "authors" artistically gave unity to their work through, among others, the following techniques: (1) inclusio (i.e., marking off a literary unity by matching the end with the beginning); (2) structures of many patterns, such as alternating (ABC::A'B'C') or chiastic (ABC X C'B'A' [i.e., the sequences before and after the turning point (called "the pivot") often contrast with one another]); (3) catch words that stitch the work together; (4) key words that focus its meaning; (5) synonyms; (6) paronomasia (i.e., a play on sound and/or sense); (7) syntax; (8) refrains; (9) janus (i.e., linking sections together with a piece of literature that looks both backward and forward); (10) contrasts and comparisons; (11) logic (e.g., cause and effect); (13) generalization; (14) preparation/foreshadow (i.e., inclusion of material in one part of the text that serves primarily to prepare the reader for what is still to come. By matching the poetic techniques embedded with the deep structure of meaning, one can discern the abstract meaning that enriches the whole, which is greater than the sum of its parts.

This new breed reads the Old Testament in a way that more closely resembles that of the rabbis than of source critics, but, unlike the ingenious rabbis, they ground their readings in the science of poetics. To be sure, good readers have always, consciously or unconsciously, used poetics to interpret a unified text. The grammar of poetics, however, brings to light that biblical authors deftly used these techniques to unify disparate sources. The fragmentary appearance of their final compositions is only skin deep; poetics shows they had in mind "big ideas" that transcend the isolated sources.

An Exposition of Proverbs 26:1–12

Let us return to our cameo to illustrate how poetics helps uncover the big idea. The larger context of Proverbs 26:9–10 is Proverbs 26:1–12. The key word uniting the composition is "fool."[3] It occurs in every verse except verse 2, which is a proverbial pair with verse 1. At verse 13, the topic shifts from the fool to the sluggard (26:13–16). The key word "fool" gave rise to the title "A Mirror of Fools"[4] for this composition, but a single word like "fool" only "masquerades" as a big idea.[5]

Formally, the composition consists of ten sayings (vv. 1–3, 6–12) and two admonitions (vv. 4–5). Apart from the concluding verse, these ten sayings have essentially the same structure. Their A versets (i.e., the first halves of the verses) present striking negative images from the order of creation to serve as a metaphor of the fool in the social order. "A Mirror of Fools" consists of an introduction, which sounds the theme (vv. 1–3); a body, which develops its two sides (vv. 4–10); and a conclusion (vv. 11–12).[6]

Introduction (vv. 1–3)

Verse 1 functions as a summarization that the body will particularize; it sounds the composition's major theme: "honor is not fitting for a fool."[7] The images of snow in summer and rain in harvest illustrate that honoring a fool occurs in a world out of joint and that to do so is catastrophic. As snow in harvest destroys crops and brings death, an individual or society that honors a fool destroys a life or a culture full of promise.

Verse 2 functions as a comparison and a contrast with verse 1. Uniquely sharing the same syntax as verse 1,[8] it too pertains to what is unfitting vis-à-vis uttering a curse against an innocent person. However, it principally functions as a contrast. On the one hand, glory is not fitting for a fool, because as verse 1 made clear (and the body will make even more clear), giving him social standing will cause great damage. On the other hand, uttering a curse against an innocent person is unfitting but will do no damage, because it has no place to land. A paronomasia (i.e., a play on sound and/or sense) assists the contrast. Hebrew *kabed*, the root of "glory" [*kabod*], means "heavy," and Hebrew *qalal*, the root of "curse" [*qelalah*], means "light." Indeed, in the Semitic languages it can mean "to be flighty," a notion that gives rise to the image of birds flying about without landing.

Verse 3 functions as a climax to the introduction and sounds the positive counterpoint to the negative theme. What is fitting is "a rod for the backs of fools"! (v. 3). The assonance, a form of paronomasia, among *sippor* ("sparrow"), *deror* ("swallow"),[9] and *hamor* ("donkey") helps sound both the positive thesis, what is fitting (v. 3), and the negative, what is unfitting (vv. 1–2). In sum, the introduction sounds the thesis along with its counterpoint.

Body: Section 1 (vv. 4–5)

Two admonitions that develop the countertheme of what is fitting for a fool logically form a relatively smooth transition from the introduction to the body. In addition to physically caning the fool to control him, without naming who is responsible (v. 3), the wise son/disciple needs to give the fool a verbal answer (vv. 4–5). His answer, however, must distinguish between what is unfitting (v. 4) and what is fitting (v. 5). It is unfitting to answer with the fool's insolence; the son must not meet "insult with insult" (1 Peter 3:9). Should he reply vindictively, harshly, or with lies—the way fools talk—he too—"yes, even you"—would come under the fool's condemnation. Rather, without lowering himself to the fool's level, and by overcoming evil with good (25:21f.), he must expose the fool's folly for what it is. The wise must not silently accept and tolerate the folly and thereby confirm fools in it.

Body: Section 2 (vv. 6–10)

The five sayings of verses 6–10 return to the introduction's form, using negative images from the created order to develop the negative and major theme. These sayings answer the questions of what is meant by "honor" and why it is "unfitting" for fools. However, they escalate the standards of comparison to striking and ludicrous images to develop the proposition.[10] Instead of drawing images from the impersonal weather (v. 1) and animals (vv. 2–3), these images are drawn from the human realm, from deformed (vv. 6–7) and deranged (vv. 9–10) people. At the pivot stands the absurd stone-slinger (v. 8).

Verses 6 and 7, in addition to the sensible binding of images pertaining to deformed people, are also connected by the images of "feet" [*raglayim*] and "legs" [*shoqayim*]. Both images uniquely share the same syntax, the Hebrew dual number. Verses 8 and 9, in addition to the sensible binding of images pertaining to deranged people, are also connected by the paronomasia of "drunkard" (*shikkor*) and "one who hires" (*shoker*). However, it is now clear the paronomasia assists the sensible binding!

Duane Garrett shows that the compilers arranged these sayings in a chiasm.[11]

A: Committing important business to a fool (v. 6)
   B: A proverb in a fool's mouth (v. 7)
      C: Honoring a fool (v. 8)
   B': A proverb in a fool's mouth (v. 9)
A': Committing important business to a fool (v. 10)

The compilers profile the chiasm by repeating verbatim in its inner core "a proverb in the mouth of a fool," an exaggerated form of catchwords, on either side of the pivot. Its outer core pertains to hiring the fool for a job, of which commissioning him to send messages is one.

In the light of this chiasm, it becomes clear that verse 8 is the pivot and that this focal verse, also the center verse of the body and conclusion, restates with increased volume the composition's big idea: "to honor a fool [is unfitting]." The decibel volume is increased by the pivot's final catchwords, "honor for/to a fool" (*lekesil kabod*), repeating verbatim the final words of the summary statement (v. 1). The absurd stone-slinger images the prosaic "not fitting" of the summarization (v. 1). Instead of hurling the stone (i.e., the fool) far from him, the ludicrous slinger (i.e., the one giving the fool honor) binds up "the stone" so that it comes around and whacks him a good one on his own head. The syntax of verse 8—*k* "like" + *ken* "so"—increases the decibel volume still further. Finally, in addition to these lexical, syntactical, and thematic links, the assonance, a form of paronomasia, of *sippor* ("sparrow"), *deror* ("swallow"), and *seror* ("binding"), turns up the volume of the restatement full blast.

In addition to focusing the composition's theme, the B versets around the pivot illuminate how one honors fools. Their inner core points to putting proverbs in their mouths (vv. 7, 9) and their outer frame to commissioning or hiring them (vv. 6, 10).[12] Turning first to the motif of "proverb" [*mashal*], note this is the most honorific term for a wise saying; it is used otherwise only of Solomon's proverbs (1:1; 10:1; 25:1). Other wise sayings are called "the sayings of the wise" (cf. 1:6; 22:17; 24:23; 30:1; 31:1). Turning to the commissioning motif, one should note that in the ancient Near East to receive a commission to represent a dignitary was a high honor indeed. In that world, the messenger was in fact the sender's plenipotentiary (i.e., vested with his full authority). However, honoring the fool with any kind of service is dangerous. In sum, one can glorify a fool by giving him an education in proverbs or by hiring him.

Finally, the A versets of the saying around the pivot elaborate why it is unfitting to honor fools. These images escalate the danger of honoring fools from hurting oneself (vv. 6–7) to hurting society at large (vv. 9–10).

The images of chopping off one's feet (v. 6) and of dangling legs (v. 7) signify respectively that giving a fool honor hurts the giver and makes the educated fool look ridiculous. Sending messages by the hand of a fool is as bizarre as chopping off one's feet and as deadly as drinking poison. By infuriating the recipient of the messages, rather than gaining a pair of feet to add to one's own, the effect is precisely the opposite, tantamount to rendering one lame.

Moreover, a proverb in the fool's mouth (v. 7), which probably got there through his improper education, is absurd and worthless. As a lame person still has legs, but cannot use them for locomotion because they hang loosely and uncertainly from his body, so proverbs in the mouths of fools carry no weight and get them nowhere. A proverb aims to involve the audience to exercise their imagination to forge a connection between the proverb's moral truth and their situation and by so doing to change their behavior. The otherwise excellent proverb, which the fool inappropriately acquired (17:16),[13] is impotent in the mouth of fools. Fools are either morally too dull to utter it seasonably, or "they invalidate its effect by their character."[14]

However, worse than being absurd and worthless (vv. 6–7), the wrongly honored fool is dangerous, even *deadly* dangerous, to society at large (vv. 9–10). He is like a drunkard[15] with a thorn bush and a mad archer. In Proverbs 20:1, intoxicants are personified as a mocker and a brawler. A thorn bush in the drunkard's hands is like the proverbial firearms in the hand of a child.[16] Today, we say, "If you drink, don't drive."[17] A proverb in the mouth of the wise brings healing, but in the mouth of a fool, it wounds and lacerates. The utterances of fools or of wicked people are dangerous (10:32; 11:9, 11; 12:18; 13:16b; 14:3 passim), but even worse, fools use the otherwise wise and excellent proverbs they learned for destructive ends.[18]

To suggest the deadly danger of educating or hiring a fool, the compiler now heightens the image from the brawling drunkard waving his thorn bush to a berserk archer shooting arrows. This dangerous character, like a modern terrorist, randomly kills all within his sight and range. Giving honor to a fool is "unfitting," to say the least!

Conclusion (vv. 11–12)

Hebrew syntax may mark off the new section. Initial *k* occurs only in verse 11, the introduction (vv. 1–2), and the pivot (v. 8) (pace NIV). Be that as it may, the last two sayings, verses 11–12, draw to conclusion "A Mirror of Fools." An inclusio connects the first of them (v. 11) with the introduction. Like verses 1–2, this saying derives its negative image from the realm of animals (sparrow/swallow [v. 2], horse/donkey [v. 3], and dog [v. 11]), not from the human sphere (vv. 6–10). The second (v. 12) is connected with the body by the catchwords "wise in his own eyes" (v. 5). That connection suggests the conclusion, like the admonitions, elaborates the composition's positive countertheme that discipline is fitting for a fool.

Verse 11 asserts that the fool cannot save himself. Using an alternate pattern (ABC::A'B'C') the saying juxtaposes a fool with the contemptible dog; his destructive folly with the dog's vomit; and the fool's obduracy with the dog's repulsive nature to return to vomit, to sniff at it, to lick it, and finally to devour it. In both the image (i.e., the dog) and the topic (i.e., the fool), the body rejects the repulsive objects (i.e., vomit and folly, respectively), but the debased spirit of the dog and fool crave them. Food poison does not affect their appetites (15:14; 17:10; 27:22).

Verse 11 pilloried the fool as incapable of saving himself because he so craves his folly that he cannot learn from his mistakes. Verse 12 opens wider a door of hope for his salvation through physical punishment and wise answers. The sages cracked that door open by suggesting a rod is fitting for a fool (v. 3). They cracked the door farther ajar by the admonition to rebut the fool wisely, before he becomes "wise in his own eyes." In this conclusion, they open the door of hope as wide as they dare. The "run-of-the-mill fool" (Garrett) has one hindrance— his ethical folly; the deluded fool has two—his folly and his conceit. The final saying offers more hope of salvation for the former than for the latter. The combined sayings (vv. 3, 4–5, 11–12) suggest that although the fool cannot learn from his mistakes, possibly he can be saved by timely, wise correction.

Verse 12 also functions as a janus to the next composition. The sages signal they are about to leave the fool behind for a new topic by dropping the structure of the preceding sayings. Instead of using negative images drawn from the created order as standards for evaluating the fool, they now use the fool as a standard of comparison for one who is wise in his own eyes. The saying shifts the son's gaze away from the fool to the sluggard who has castled himself in his own conceit.

Conclusion

The passage's big idea can now be stated. It is unfitting, downright dangerous, for the sake of everyone to honor a fool by educating him with proverbs and entrusting him with responsible service, but fitting to punish and rebuke him.

I deliberately chose a text from the Book of Proverbs because it is most difficult to apply Haddon Robinson's method of preaching to this obvious anthology. If poetics can serve as a handmaid to his thesis in this anthology that lacks syndetic markers (e.g., "and," "because," "therefore," etc.), the logic of a fortiori suggests it can, and possibly does, serve anywhere in the Old Testament. However, poetics works best with the Hebrew text. Unfortunately, the translators of the English versions of the Bible—of whom I confess to be one—are not as literate as the original audiences were. The authors of the Old Testament presumed an audience that could identify their subtle clues to meaning and rightly interpret their texts, but translators only now are beginning to pick them up.

There is a flip side to the big idea of our sample text vis-à-vis it is fitting to honor the wise, and blessings pronounced upon him find a landing place. This flip side is another reason I chose this text. This essay aims to honor my esteemed friend, Haddon Robinson, whose name has become synonymous with the theory of combining propositional preaching with exposition. However, one has to read this small contribution in light of the whole book to see the point.

For Further Reflection

Getting the Idea

1. What is this chapter talking about?
2. What is this chapter saying about what it's talking about?

Building on the Idea

1. What are the elements of poetic artistry and how can the preacher treat them in developing the sermon?

2. When dealing with poetics, with what must the "big idea" preacher be aware?
3. What is the role of literary source criticism in preparing to preach?

Recommended Reading

Alter, Robert. *The Art of Biblical Narrative.* New York: Basic Books, 1981.

Alter, Robert, and Frank Kermode, eds. *The Literary Guide to the Bible.* Cambridge, Mass.: Belknap, 1987.

Berlin, Adele. *Poetics and Interpretation of Biblical Literature.* JSOT, Supplements Series; Bible and Literature Series, no. 9. Sheffield, England: Almond, 1983.

Greidanus, Sidney. *The Modern Preacher and the Ancient Text: Interpreting and Preaching Biblical Literature.* Grand Rapids: Eerdmans, 1988.

Long, Thomas. *Preaching and the Literary Forms of the Bible.* Philadelphia: Fortress, 1989.

Longman, Tremper, III. *Literary Approaches to Biblical Interpretation.* Grand Rapids: Zondervan, 1987.

4

New Testament Challenges to Big Idea Preaching

Duane Litfin

For more than three decades I have had the privilege of calling Haddon Robinson my teacher, mentor, colleague, and, best of all, friend. Over the years we have spent countless hours talking about preaching. About everything else, too, but somehow, the subject always comes back to preaching. Most of what I know about the subject I have learned from Haddon Robinson.

Based on those decades of working with Haddon Robinson, I want to identify some of the unique challenges we face when we attempt to do expository preaching—of the sort espoused by him—from the New Testament. But first I must make a confession, and offer what I consider some important clarifications.

A Confession

It may be tempting when one thinks of Haddon Robinson's homiletical approach to conjure up creative outlines, captivating supporting material, and scintillating language, all delivered with flawless timing and dramatic flourish, because this is what we typically get when we hear him preach. But while his ability to produce such things, in himself and others, is legendary, we may for the moment put these features aside, because they are not what distinguish his homiletical theory. Nor are they what people normally have in mind when they speak of his approach as "big idea" preaching.

The distinguishing mark of his approach to preaching lies in the creative and single-minded way Haddon Robinson has worked out two fundamental commitments that lay at the core of his theory of homiletics. Others through the years have paid homage to these same commitments, but none more effectively, it seems to me, than Haddon Robinson.

The first of these commitments is to expository preaching.

Robinson's abiding commitment to exposition grows out of the church's ancient conviction that the Bible is the ever-reliable inscripturated Word of God and, as such, is the Christian's "only rule of faith and practice." This age-old claim suggests that preaching, to be all that it should be, must be expository. That is, if we are truly to preach the Word of God, the substance of our preaching should be both derived from and—here is the kicker—transmitted through the study of a passage of the Bible. This is what it means to say a sermon is expository.

Robinson's second basic commitment is to effective communication.

Long ago Haddon Robinson began a lifetime study of human communication. From this study emerged an understanding of one of the field's most important insights: we humans typically think and communicate in ideas, which we transmit to one another in what we may call "units of discourse."

The smallest unit of discourse is the simple, grammatically complete, declarative sentence. Such a sentence constitutes by definition a single idea; it consists of something being predicated about something else. These smallest units we typically organize—at least when we are communicating effectively—into larger units such as paragraphs, sections, pericopes, or stanzas, depend-

54

ing on the genre of communication we have chosen. Moreover, each of these larger units—again, when we are organizing our thoughts most effectively—will have its own unifying idea. This is in fact what renders them "units." In other words, it is precisely the presence of a central idea that provides each unit its "unit-y," its "unit-ness," so to speak.

If this seems forbiddingly abstract and complex, we may be comforted by the fact that we are well-schooled in dealing with such units of discourse, since this is what we do whenever we use language to communicate with one another. It is, in fact, what is taking place at this moment, as I attempt to organize the various units of discourse you see before you into a pattern you can understand.

It is even more likely, on the other hand, that I have made a complicated subject sound too simple. Given our lack of time and space, that is inevitable. Yet the core insight stands. In fact, it is just this insight which for millennia has led some of history's most astute observers of human behavior to note that effective communicators tend to organize their speeches around, not a random batch of ideas, but a single, significant, "central" idea. Effective speakers design their efforts to accommodate this insight, with the result that they enhance their audience's ability to understand.

This is the principle that undergirds that dimension of Haddon Robinson's teaching that has attracted the label "big idea" preaching. When combined with the foregoing commitment to Scripture, the two lead naturally to several conclusions.

First, because God chose to communicate his inscripturated revelation in the form of ordinary human language, that communication of necessity will consist of organized units of discourse. Thus, to understand that revelation we must discern these units and discover the ideas they embody.

Second, if we are to communicate effectively with our audience, our own messages should also be the embodiment of a central idea.

Third, if that idea is to bear the authority of Heaven, it must be an idea "derived from" and, ideally, "transmitted through" the study of a biblical passage in its context.

Fourth, the biblical passage one chooses for an expository sermon must not be merely a random grouping of verses, but a valid unit of discourse. A random group of verses would, by definition, be without a central idea. So any attempt to preach a central idea from such a passage would of necessity fail to do justice to the text. On the other hand, a legitimate unit of discourse is marked by the fact that it embodies a central idea. Thus it follows that a faithful exposition of that passage will also display a central idea.

If we are to handle the text of Scripture with integrity, Haddon Robinson has taught us, we must listen to it at the level of its ideas. This means that we must discern and deal carefully with the units of discourse that make up the Bible's text. Conversely, if we are also to communicate effectively with our own audiences, our messages must also consist of clear units of discourse, each with its own central idea. Happily, these two necessities work in close synergy, because they stem from the same basic insight into how human beings use language. The expositor's sermon constitutes a unit of discourse—that is, a more or less elaborate development of a single, significant idea—because it consists of an exposition of a biblical unit of discourse.

Haddon Robinson would be the first to insist that he is not alone in either his emphasis on exposition or his stress on dealing with complete ideas. Far from inventing these emphases, it is his contention that these represent the best thinking of the centuries, which he is merely interpreting afresh to his own generation. That he has done so more effectively than most will not be debated by any who have studied with him. But it is important to remember that what he offers us is neither a gimmick, nor some trendy method, nor yet merely one more approach among many. What he offers is the creative application of fundamental principles. It is just this that gives his teaching such substance.

Ten Challenges to New Testament Exposition

As Haddon Robinson's students will testify, this sort of preaching throws up many challenges, which we will face whether our passage is drawn from the Old or the New Testament.

For instance, whatever one's passage, this kind of preaching requires clear and rigorous thought. As Robinson sometimes says, "Thinking is hard work, and thinking about thinking is even harder work." The exposition we are talking about requires heavy doses of both. Wrestling ourselves clear with an author's thought, and then wrestling ourselves clear with our own, is not for the mentally lazy. It often involves long hours of struggle in order to understand and capture fully and accurately what an author is saying; then equally long hours struggling to produce a message that will communicate that message, and its implications, faithfully and creatively to our own audience. It can be an exhausting task.

Moreover, this is an area where standard commentaries often provide little aid. If we need insight into the historical background of a passage, or some technical aspect of its grammar, or the etymology of a key term, commentaries will often be a wonderful source of help. But how many commentaries provide, for example, detailed full-sentence outlines of the biblical text, outlines that lay out the author's thought in the form of complete ideas, unit by unit? This common shortcoming leaves to expositors the difficult task of working through to those full ideas on their own.

Some of our challenges, however, are unique to specific parts of the Bible. The following is not an exhaustive list, nor are some of these items without their counterparts in the Old Testament. Yet below are ten of the most common challenges "central idea expositors" encounter when preaching the New Testament.

1. The Absence of Textual Dividers in the Original

We have said that the determination of the biblical unit of discourse is crucial to the task of exposition, for from this decision will flow our understanding of the author's central idea as well as our own. But sometimes the biblical units of discourse can be difficult to discern. One of the reasons for this is the lack of punctuation or textual dividers in the original documents.

Modern readers take punctuation and textual dividers for granted since they are an inherent part of all we read. But the Greek of the biblical texts carried minimal punctuation and few such dividers. It consisted of a stream of letters readers were to divide for themselves into appropriate units.

For the most part, the original readers knew intuitively where to place such divisions so as to "rightly divide" the author's ideas. Modern readers, by contrast, often lack these intuitions. Fortunately, this shortcoming can be largely offset by the application of exegetical skill, experience, and hard work. Gaining this skill and experience, and then expending the effort to apply them to specific texts, constitutes one of the expositor's most important challenges.

2. The Presence of Mistaken Textual Dividers

To help relieve the above problem, various dividers have been built into the text of the Bible over the years. The chapter and verse divisions are centuries old and tend to be standardized for modern readers, but the paragraph and sectional divisions still vary somewhat according to the Greek or English version one is using. These divisions were placed in the text by competent people who typically had given the matter much prayer, study, and, often, debate. Thus these dividers usually represent the author's thought accurately and help the modern reader grasp the flow of ideas. But there is a potential downside as well.

Since in most cases the division represents a judgment someone other than the author has made, these divisions cannot be treated as if they bear the authority of the original. Sometimes such divisions prove less than helpful, and on occasion they are simply wrong. Divisions that were designed to aid us wind up obscuring or distorting the author's thought rather than revealing it.

For example, a comparison of Hebrews 10:19–25 and Hebrews 12:1–3 might suggest that the chapter break after Hebrews

12:28–29 is very poorly placed. In such cases unfortunate textual divisions present the expositor with a twofold problem: first, they make it more difficult to see the text with fresh eyes, apart from the mistaken divider; second, they make effective exposition more difficult, since the audience already has the division in front of them. Yet, because the accurate determination of the author's units of discourse is so important, the "central idea expositor" must come to the text willing to evaluate the options, grasp the reasons for the division, and, on occasion, overrule an editorial decision.

3. Exegetical Ambiguities

Like any language, Koine Greek had built-in nuances that only a fluent native speaker would immediately grasp. Today we can recover many of these nuances only through hard work and shrewd exegetical judgments.

One of the most prominent examples of this is the Greek participle. Inherently ambiguous, Greek participles constitute one of the New Testament expositor's most interesting challenges. Should a given participle be interpreted temporally, causally, conditionally, or in some other fashion? In the New Testament, particularly in the epistles, our grasp of the author's thought will sometimes hinge on how we construe a single participle.

Another instance is the Greek case system. The semantic emphases of the Greek cases are more or less well understood, but this does not eliminate difficult decisions about the author's intent. A classic example is found in 2 Corinthians 5:14. When Paul uses the genitive to speak of "the love of Christ," does he mean "my love for Christ" (objective genitive) or "Christ's love for me" (subjective genitive)? What we decide on this thorny question may dramatically affect our central idea.

4. The New Testament's Use of Old Testament

Another unique challenge for the expositor is the complex question of the New Testament's use of the Old. When we come across a citation from the Old Testament, whose ideas are we exploring, the Old Testament author's or the New Testament author's? Did the New Testament authors always use the Old Testament in such a way that these ideas inevitably are the same or at least overlapping, or do the two sometimes differ? To what extent and in what ways? How does the fact that the Holy Spirit is the ultimate author of both references affect our conclusions? Homiletically, must we take a major trek with our audience back into the Old Testament in each case to do justice to the quoted material? And how are we to handle those complications that arise from the fact that New Testament authors typically quoted not from the Hebrew but from the Greek translation of the Old Testament, the Septuagint, which sometimes seems to differ from the original Hebrew?

These and similar questions have vexed students of the Bible for centuries and, despite much debate and discussion, few answers have gained universal agreement. Yet expositors, who must concern themselves with the ideas of the text, cannot simply ignore such questions. New Testament citations of the Old often add wonderful insights into both Testaments and are therefore uniquely valuable. But they can also present us with some of our most difficult expository challenges.

5. Unique Genres of Literature

To interpret any passage of Scripture accurately it is crucial to understand the type of literature we are handling. For example, the psalms are poetry and must be treated as such; they must not be handled as if they were epistolary literature like Romans. Similarly, parables are parables and are not to be treated as historical narratives. Proverbs are just that—proverbs. They should not be confused with promises. Each category, or genre, of biblical literature bears its own distinctive features and must be handled accordingly.

But this presupposes that we both understand the genre and can identify our material as belonging to that genre. On both counts expositors face a problem when it comes to the Gospels.

The four Gospels—Matthew, Mark, Luke, and John—account for over 40 percent of the New Testament. On the surface they appear to be straightforward historical narratives. But this exterior masks features that have kept scholars debating for years. How important, for example, was chronology to the Gospel writers? Are the Gospels theology through a historical grid, or history through a theological grid? In the end, it may be that the Gospels constitute a genre of their own. But what are the features of this genre, and what are the implications for how the Gospels are to be understood? Different scholars have offered contrasting answers, making the exposition of the Gospels more of a challenge for the conscientious expositor than one might guess.

6. The Presence of Secondary Voices

When we speak of the central idea of our passage, we normally mean the author's idea. But what are we to make of passages where the unit includes, but is not restricted to, sizable segments of someone else's discourse? Are we to assume that the idea of the author and that of the quoted speaker are always the same? And if not, which is to be considered the idea of the passage?

The most common examples of this dilemma occur in the Gospels, where the writer is quoting or summarizing the teaching of Jesus. Mark has designed a narrative to communicate his own point: that Jesus is the Son of God who has power over the forces of evil. Included in his narrative is material focusing on Jesus' own teaching about Satan. In preaching such a unit, would the thrust of our preaching idea be Luke's point about Jesus or Jesus' point about Satan? Sorting through these complexities can be a delicate task for the careful expositor.

7. Determining the Purpose of a New Testament Book

Understanding the writer's overall purpose is often a major help in interpreting a book of the Bible and its many subunits. For example, when at the end of his Gospel John says, "I have written these things so that you may believe that Jesus is the Christ, the Son of God, and that by believing you may have life in his name"

(20:30–31), he provides us his purpose: to present Jesus as the object of our belief. Knowing this helps us keep a clear Christocentric focus throughout our exposition of the Gospel of John.

But what if we do not know, or cannot make up our minds about, an author's purpose? A classic example of this problem is the Book of Acts. On the surface the subject matter seems straightforward enough. It is a record of the earliest spread of the gospel from its Jewish roots out into the Gentile world. But what was the purpose of the book?

Some argue that Acts was written merely to provide us with a historical account of the early years of the church. If one chooses this option, then issues of the church will play the lead throughout the exposition of the book.

Others, however, point to the first verse, where Luke notes that his "former treatise," the Gospel of Luke, was designed to focus on "all that Jesus began to do and teach." The Book of Acts, Luke's volume 2, they then point out, was seemingly designed to describe all that Jesus continued to do and teach, now through his apostles. With this reading, the focus of the exposition shifts somewhat to showing how the risen Christ was at work in all that Acts records.

Still others have argued that Acts was written as a quasi-legal document to be used in Paul's trial in Rome. According to this reading, the purpose of Acts was to provide a witness in Rome and show that the charges against Paul were false. With this reading, the ministry of Paul might move to the forefront.

These and other views of the purpose of Acts are not necessarily mutually exclusive. Yet our reading of Luke's purpose will have a shaping effect on how we expound Luke's text. If we were not dealing so rigorously at the level of the text's ideas, understanding a book's purpose might be less significant. It is the requirements of "big idea" exposition that bring such questions to the fore.

8. The Lack of a Central Idea

We have said that effective communicators tend to organize their ideas into units of discourse, which by definition are bodies of text that have a central idea. The smallest units (sentences) are built into larger units (paragraphs, sections, etc.), which in turn make up the entire unit (in the Bible, a book). Thus we would expect to be able to outline an entire book of the Bible, in full sentence form, from its most basic units up to the overall unit, the book itself. Conversely, we would expect each book of the Bible to display a central idea which, in turn, is developed by each of its subunits. This is, at least in theory, what we would expect.

Yet some books of the Bible seem to defy our search for their central idea. Their subunits are each coherent enough, but try as we might we are unable to see how all of the major subunits fit together to develop a single, central idea for the book as a whole. An example of this is the Book of James.

James is for many a favorite book of the Bible. While it develops few of the great theological themes of the Bible, it is intensely practical and life-related. But what is the book's central idea? It deals with subjects such as temptation, the tongue, wisdom, and worldliness, in subunits which each yield more or less clear central ideas. But do those subunits combine to develop an overall central idea? And if not, what does that say about the importance of designing our messages around a single, significant idea? If James does not do it, why must we?

There are those who will argue that the Book of James does display a central idea, but we shall not join that debate here. We need only observe that our stress on the need for a central idea must always be qualified; it is not an absolute. To be sure, we cannot communicate or even think apart from that basic building block, the complete thought. But we can communicate, and even communicate effectively, without building those basic units into an overall unit. For example, we may write a perfectly useful letter to a friend without worrying about designing it around a central idea. Or James may be a useful book even if it does not possess a central idea.

Yet the principle holds true. A communicational effort built around a single, central idea tends to be more effective. This can be seen by the fact that most of the books of the Bible do in fact display a central idea, and even by the fact that James would be an easier book to understand and teach if it had a clearly discernible central idea as well. As it is, James presents the expositor some genuine challenges in discerning how the parts of his letter fit together.

9. Long Sentences

Another New Testament challenge for central idea exposition are the long run-on sentences one sometimes finds in the Greek. Consider, for example, the famous sentence found in Ephesians 1:3–14.

This single Pauline sentence consists of a skein of ideas compounded into a long and complex grammatical structure. To render these ideas more accessible, most English translations separate this extended sentence into a series of shorter sentences. The New International Version, for instance, divides this chain of ideas into no fewer than seven shorter sentences, each of which themselves remain relatively long and complex by English standards. Moreover, the substance of these Pauline ideas qualifies as some of the deepest to be found anywhere in the New Testament. Needless to say, unpacking for an audience this tangle of profound ideas, in such a way as to do justice to both their substance and their relationships to one another, represents a daunting task for the "big idea" expositor.

10. Lists of Exhortations

The opposite problem occurs in New Testament sections that consist of a list of single, relatively undeveloped exhortations, each of which constitutes an individual idea. For example, in 1 Thessalonians 5:12–22, in a section the NIV can only label "Final Instructions," the Apostle Paul offers no fewer than seventeen distinct exhortations in only ten verses. Each of these exhortations represents separate ideas. Yet they do not naturally add up to any overall central idea. In an attempt to help matters, the NIV has divided the section into three paragraphs. But beyond the desire to render the section less dense, the reasoning behind the paragraph divisions is not clear; they do not appear to be justified by any logical groupings of these exhortations.

How, then, does an expositor who is determined to deal with the ideas of the text preach through such material? One might preach a single sermon on each exhortation, or perhaps one could preach the entire list (or segments of the list) while foregoing a central idea to the sermon. Either of these options might work. But those committed to genuine exposition would avoid the common mistake of forcing some foreign organizing principle onto the whole or parts.

Conclusion

It was said of Ezra, one of our expository forefathers, that he "had set his heart to study the law of the LORD and to practice it, and to teach His statutes and ordinances in Israel" (Ezra 7:10). No one, least of all Haddon Robinson, ever said following in Ezra's footsteps would or should be easy.

When we do exposition we are dealing with the inscripturated Word of God, which has been delivered to us from another time and place in a complicated mix of poems, stories, letters, proverbs, histories, or prophecies. Yet all these forms and more are dealing in one way or another with ideas—in fact, the most important ideas in the world. For the expositor there is no way around the challenges we will encounter in attempting to preach these ideas. It is our calling and our privilege, as it was with Ezra, to study these truths and practice them, and then teach them faithfully to God's people.

For Further Reflection

Getting the Idea

1. What is this chapter talking about?
2. What is this chapter saying about what it's talking about?

Building on the Idea

1. List the ten challenges to New Testament exposition faced by "big idea" expositors.
2. Compare the list of ten challenges with a New Testament passage you are currently preparing to preach. What are the difficulties you find and how will you deal with them as you prepare your message?
3. Why is it important to deal with a clear unit of discourse when preaching?

Recommended Reading

Craddock, Fred B. *Preaching.* Nashville: Abingdon, 1985.

Davis, H. Grady. *Design for Preaching.* Philadelphia: Fortress, 1958.

Litfin, Duane. *Public Speaking: A Handbook for Christians,* 2nd ed. Grand Rapids: Baker, 1992.

Osborne, Grant R. *The Hermeneutical Spiral: A Comprehensive Introduction to Biblical Interpretation.* Downers Grove: InterVarsity, 1992.

Wilson, John F., and Carroll C. Arnold. *Public Speaking as a Liberal Art.* 3rd ed. Boston: Allyn & Bacon, 1974.

5

Is There Really One Big Idea in That Story?

Paul Borden

Introduction

When Mommy or Daddy began, "Once upon a time . . . ," we listened. We learned early that stories caused us to stop what we were doing and to pay attention to the storyteller. Instinctively we knew we lived life in narrative. Story, like breathing or thinking, is an intrinsic part of our existence. We daydream, plot, criticize, hope, and visualize ambitions in story form. No one lives life deductively.

Perhaps this is why our Creator designed much of biblical revelation to be written in story form. Jesus Christ, who preached didactic sermons and taught deductively, was also well known for his stories. The human authors God employed to instruct the church about Jesus Christ's life and ministry thought it wise to choose story as their predominate means of communication.

Yet today the preponderance of sermons, especially those preached by individuals who champion biblical authority and integrity, are not given in story form and are seldom based on narrative passages. There often appears to be a studied avoidance of narrative combined with a rhetorical form that communicates ineffectively to audiences saturated by an electronic media.

I believe there are at least two major reasons for this paradox. First, preachers are convinced that abstract truth cannot be communicated well in story form. Second, many preachers are not trained to discover the big idea of a story and then communicate that story without violating the narrative genre.

The reason preachers often fail to value stories as media of theological and biblical truth is that our literate technological culture has convinced us that truth cannot be communicated in this manner. Stories may be used to illustrate truth but not communicate it. One example of this belief is the approach used to teach history. To understand the political foundations of American history, students are encouraged to study the writings of Thomas Jefferson or read the Federalist Papers or the treaties of Locke and Rousseau. Narrative historical accounts, anecdotes, and eyewitness descriptions only provide illustrations of the concepts and ideas contained in such volumes. However, these stories do not and cannot be used to communicate ideas. The crucial ideas can only be communicated analytically and logically, not narratively!

While analytical and logical presentations are sometimes required and beneficial, the assumption behind such presentations is often one of disdain for narrative as the means for communicating major ideas.

Yet often the same preachers who by choice of materials (didactic literature) and preaching style (deductive presentations) confirm this bias, decry the corruption of the national culture. Their sermons often condemn declining morality, unwise choices and spiritual bankruptcy. A major culprit often cited for contributing to this decline is "the media," that is, television, radio, movies, and music.

Facing a Contradiction

If this analysis of culture is correct, and a significant force contributing to this current decline is "the media," then these preachers are faced with a contradiction: stories permeate all mass media from television, including commercials, to movies and music. Now I admit that the declining values, improper attitudes, and inverted priorities reflected in stories come from reasoned arguments and well-articulated ideas of secular philosophers. However, more people in the culture are influenced, not by the papers and books of the philosophers, ethicists, or commentators, but rather by the artistic communication of their ideas in the media. While people are laughing, crying, and identifying with real-life stories in drama and music, they are adopting values that contribute to a declining cultural morality. In other words, it is the stories and the ideas taught by stories that influence people more often than the scholarly presentations of those same ideas articulated in speeches and papers.

Preachers should recognize that the screenwriter and director do more to influence today's North American culture than the philosopher. Perhaps this is why story seems to be God's favorite medium of written revelation. Perhaps he understood that the storyteller communicates truth more widely than the theologian.

The second reason many preachers either avoid stories or handle them poorly is due to poor modeling and training. In the past, preachers tended to treat stories as allegories or illustrations of preconceived theological ideas gained from didactic passages. Such preachers did not understand narrative literature and were not taught to interpret it. This lack of training continues to the present. Seminaries seldom if ever offer required courses in the exegesis and preaching of stories. Most require exegetical courses focused on didactic material, which do not train students to understand and communicate narrative literature. In fact, frequently the methodologies that enable us to understand didactic literature inhibit us from understanding narrative literature. I would go one step further and contend that Greek exegesis is

69

simply one form of special hermeneutics that enables us to understand only didactic material.

One example of the inability of poorly trained preachers to handle narrative is the constant inconsistency of turning description into prescription. As we repeatedly listen to several sermons on the same narrative passage, we hear numerous interpretations. Whereas different sermons on Romans 5 may illustrate, develop, and apply the concept of headship quite individually, the basic exegesis remains the same. Perhaps the debate over the lordship of Christ, which seems to raise its head periodically, does so because many of the key passages are found in narrative texts.

In light of these observations, I would like to offer an exegetical method designed to discover the big ideas communicated in biblical stories. I also want to suggest a way to preach these stories in current-day homiletical styles that will not violate the truth of the story or its development in narrative genre. This does not mean that I have to preach narrative in story form. However, I must be assured I do not violate the narrative form in the way I preach the story.

Some Important Assumptions

Important assumptions underlie this exegetical method. The first assumption relates to the historical orthodox position of inspiration, which holds that God and humans were both extensively and equally involved in the production of Scripture. This means that when God chose to reveal truth through narratives, he selected highly competent storytellers. These individuals developed this form of literature artfully and skillfully.

The result of making this assumption that God selected skillful storytellers is that we interpreters cannot violate the essence of good narrative when exegeting text. Stories are not like didactic literature that can be taken apart verse by verse or paragraph by paragraph. Each story is a unit, whether it is a paragraph long (as in the Gospels) or a chapter or two long (as in the Old Testament). To preach fifteen verses out of a story that is fifty verses long violates the essence of story. It is like reading children the middle of a bedtime story without telling them how the story began or ended. The result is to preach an idea that may be true but is not based on the teaching of that narrative.

The second assumption is that the narrative portions of the Scripture were not written primarily to provide a record of redemptive history. This is not to say that these stories are historically inaccurate; they are quite accurate. An orthodox view of inspiration argues for historical accuracy. However, the primary purpose of the narratives was to develop a theology through story, not create a historical record. This understanding of narratives seems to be borne out by New Testament comments about Old Testament stories (Rom. 15:4; 1 Cor. 10:11; 2 Tim. 3:16; Heb. 1:1, 2). It is also demonstrated in any comparison of the four Gospels.

There are several crucial results related to the assumption that narratives were not written primarily to record history. First, narratives were written to communicate a theology. This means that each narrative book has as well defined an argument as Romans or any other New Testament epistle. The difference is that each book's argument is developed by a series of stories while Romans is developed through a logical, analytical presentation. Often our inability to recognize this is due to our assumptions coupled with our inability to exegete story as story. Second, an overall chronology is seldom the concern of the storyteller since the purpose is to develop a theological argument, not record a chronological history. If chronology is crucial, the storyteller notes it; otherwise chronology is usually ignored. Older debates over the Bible's authenticity based on chronological issues reflected the fact that both sides assumed that the purpose of narratives was to record history rather than develop an argument. The third implication is to see what the narratives have in common, even though narratives may be separated by years. Therefore, outlines of narrative books should reflect theological developments rather than historical, geographical, or biographical concerns. Again, our understanding the Gospels should convince us that this is true. Knowing Old Testament history is important, but often teaching the Old Testament as history does a disservice to future interpreters. It plants false assumptions.

The fourth assumption underlying this method of exegesis is that each narrative communicates a big idea that is unique. Stories, like other biblical literature, contribute to the grand ideas of Scripture. However, each story offers its own unique facet and insight into one of those grand ideas.

The implication of the assumption that each narrative is unique in its teaching means that the idea preached from one narrative fits no other narrative. If a sermon preached from one narrative could be used with a different one, then the preacher's understanding of one or both narratives is incorrect. An infinite God who creates unique personalities, snowflakes, and fingerprints has done the same with stories, including those accounts that are parallel.

This assumption opens up the narratives as never before. Too often our thinking has been confined to just a few themes, while in reality God has placed a wealth of biblical ideas in stories. I frequently find myself addressing issues that are not developed anywhere else in Scripture, except through application.

The last assumption is that the major moral, spiritual, or theological truth of the narrative can only be understood when one understands the entire story. Other moral, ethical, or theological issues raised in the story may not, and in fact often will not, be addressed by the storyteller.

The implications of the assumption that each story generally speaks to one major issue while ignoring others means that we as preachers must do the same. To focus on other issues either positively or negatively is to treat narrative like allegory. Outlining stories chronologically (as we many times do with the epistles) also treats story as allegory and not as story. We must exegete narratives to discover the major truth, and then focus on that truth in preaching while ignoring other issues not developed in the narrative.

The Exegetical Method

We must first determine where the story begins and ends. This is not always easy to do. Narrative books are like novels. In each one there are several smaller books that make up one complete volume. For example, the Book of Genesis has included in it the book of Abraham, the book of Isaac, and the book of Jacob. Within each of these books are chapters or narratives. These narratives may take in one, two, or three biblical chapters. That means that current chapter divisions are often meaningless in determining individual narratives. Therefore I must read several narratives a number of times, often in different translations, to determine where a particular story begins and ends. Once I have determined the beginning and ending, I need to recognize that further exegesis may require later adjustments. I am now ready to begin to exegete the story.

Designing the Story

My first responsibility is to determine the design of the story. Many stories are told in third person, while some are first-person accounts. Some stories begin at the beginning and continue on to the end, while others use flashback. Some stories place the emphasis on plot, while others focus on action or character development. As I note these observations, I am raising questions about why the story is designed as it is. However, these questions cannot be answered until the exegetical process is completed.

Next, I divide the story into scenes. It is helpful to imagine that you are a movie director shooting a story. Each scene is filmed in a certain way to tell the story, remembering that the order of scenes is important. The New American Standard Bible (NASB) paragraph divisions seem to offer the best division of scenes in the narratives.

It is most helpful to make a chart for each paragraph or scene using one large piece of blank paper. Exegetical notes, observations, questions, and so on are then written in each section of the chart that corresponds to the appropriate scene. The design of the scenes is best understood through charting.

List the Characters

Next, develop a list of characters. Again, it is helpful to compare the characters in a story to actors in a drama: "Who is the star? Who is the antagonist? Who is the protagonist? Who is the character actor crucial to the story's development? Who are the extras? Characters show us how life is lived out and managed in particular situations (the scenes). The living out of life is not announced but accomplished, sometimes successfully, sometimes unsuccessfully, in the conflict of the drama.

Then note the action. As events unfold, characters respond and act, which produces further action. In a character study the action may be thought or dialogue. But even the dialogue or thought is a reaction to events and produces further action that eventually leads to some kind of climax.

Examine Dialogue

The next step is to examine any dialogue. (Dialogue may actually be monologue; however, I am using the term "dialogue" in its broadest sense.) The major method for developing characterization in narrative is through the words spoken by the characters. The storyteller (in this case ultimately the Holy Spirit) often communicates the major idea through the words that are uttered by the characters. Many biblical stories are condensed, meaning the storyteller is functioning as an editor, which makes dialogue important. Note the dialogue to appear first in a story, or dialogue that is repeated, especially with minor variations. Such minor variations often have major significance. It is at this point that the interpreter employs lexical or grammatical processes. However, in narrative exegesis these processes are usually not needed to determine the idea. Sometimes the idea is developed more through the design, plot, action, and so on, than through the dialogue. That which makes the interpretation of narratives difficult is that the idea is seldom developed the same way in each narrative. The implementation of exegetical rules may require more artistic flair than needed for didactic materials.

List Narrator Statements

The next step in the exegetical method is to list the statements made by the narrator. Without these statements the story would not make sense because specific motives, thoughts, hidden actions, and the like would not be known. As many have noted, the narrator is omniscient, knowing thoughts, intimate and private conversations, hidden events, and God's mind. These statements are God's entrance as the ultimate storyteller into the story. Therefore, these comments become decisive in ultimately determining the meaning of the story.

Discover the Plot

Next, we must discover the plot. This is not always easy, especially if one knows the story well. Look at the story and determine those events that create and intensify the disequilibrium. Then determine where reversal occurs, changing the course established by the disequilibrium. Finally, establish how the story is resolved. In developing plot, it is important to determine whether the story is a comedy or tragedy. The events that develop the plot in a comedy may not be the ones that develop the plot in a tragedy or vice versa. We must remember that the biblical stories are not morality plays where good and evil are obvious. Stories have the ability to handle well the ambiguities of life.

Final Steps

After this, examine the tone of the story. You are seeking the worldview being communicated. The way the story is told is often as important as the story itself in determining tone.

The next step is to look for rhetorical structures. Such structures may include chiasm, repetition, contrasts, or a scene that seems out of place with other scenes. Often an anomaly in the pattern or structure points to the major idea being developed in the story. Again, just as certain scenes in movies are pivotal, so certain patterns or deviations from patterns are critical to the story's point.

Finally, the interpreter gathers data from the context. The context is the stories that surround the narrative and create a section. Often, it is best to read the narratives on each side of the one being studied and write a single descriptive sentence title for each. If each story is described accurately in the sentence title, the interpreter begins to gain a sense of how the narrative being studied fits the context. It is crucial at this time to observe how the stories develop ideas rather than focusing on chronology. Remember, narratives are grouped together to create a theological argument.

A Sentence for Each Scene and Emphasis

Following these exegetical steps, write a single descriptive sentence title for each scene or paragraph. This title should include no interpretation. Again, this is difficult. Yet our inability to deal with story as story requires this step. We must force ourselves to learn what is in the story before we begin to ask why.

Once you have written these sentences, create a single descriptive title for the entire narrative. This sentence should accurately summarize and reflect the paragraph titles. Oftentimes the idea is missed because the major elements of the narrative are not precisely described.

Observe the sentences (paragraph titles and narrative titles) and ascertain the writer's emphasis. No two stories are the same in content and presentation. In each story certain literary aspects are emphasized at the expense of others to communicate the idea. Evidence must be weighed. Sometimes the storyteller may focus on characters, dialogue, and plot. Other times the focus may be design, scene, and the narrator's comments. The formula is never the same. Finding the meaning of stories is like being a detective with a myriad of clues. Only certain clues reveal the mystery while other clues, if pursued, lead to a false conclusion. However, if the correct clues are used to uncover the crime, all the other clues fit in place. Then and only then can the interpreter begin to know the truth communicated in a particular narrative.

After you discover the storyteller's emphasis, determine what the story is about. This determination provides the subject. Then decide what is being said about the subject, since this provides the complement for the idea. Now you are ready to take the sentence descriptive title, if it has been stated accurately and precisely, and supply the interpretation. Add the interpretive elements to the descriptive elements in order to state the storyteller's idea. State this idea in one sentence and it becomes the exegetical idea of the story. When this idea is stated accurately and truthfully, it will fit this story alone and no other.

Once you have the exegetical idea, you have completed the exegesis of the narrative. This process, like all exegetical methods, is difficult. You also gain expertise in developing the exegetical idea as you find it, time after time. The important idea to remember is that the exegetical method for narratives is different from the methods used to discover God's ideas in letters, poems, proverbs, or parables.

The Homiletical Process

Movies again provide a helpful clue. We distinguish among action movies, character studies, mysteries, period pieces, and classics. A movie based on a work by Tom Wolfe will be developed quite differently than one taken from Tom Clancy. Both movies will have a basic idea to communicate, however, the director will get the idea across quite differently, just as the original author did.

Narrative passages lend themselves easily to narrative-style sermons, either in first- or third-person presentations. However, I wish to describe a process that fits the traditional format while enabling preachers to construct sermons that do not violate the essence of story in their presentations.

The Preaching Idea

First, examine the exegetical idea and determine how you can restate it so it both reflects the historical accurateness and literary intent of the story while using terms that create a timeless proposition. This process requires much effort and numerous restatements. However, once you have correctly stated the idea this way, you have the eternal theological concept that is true for God's people in any era. This is your preaching idea.

The preaching idea is the precise answer to a specific need, problem, or difficulty in life. The story you have exegeted reveals how an individual or group has dealt with this issue successfully or unsuccessfully from God's perspective. The preaching idea is the remedy; the story reveals how spiritually diseased people embraced or rejected this remedy.

Your job as the preacher is to develop for your congregation how people relate, interact, and struggle with the same spiritual disease. You pick those aspects of the story that enable you to illustrate this disease. Rather than thinking of which verses do this, demonstrate how the plot, character development, scenes, actions, design, tone, and so on develop the disease. You use these elements to state, elaborate, and build the first half to two-thirds of your sermon.

This process of developing the spiritual disease means that two things always occur. First, the sermon seldom ever follows the narrative chronologically. Second, you develop the sermon using disequilibrium. The disequilibrium of the story may be used, but more often it is the disequilibrium of the disease for which the remedy is the preaching idea.

The Remedy and Acceptance of It

Now you are ready to develop the second aspect of your sermon, the remedy. You go to the elements of the story that support the exegetical/preaching idea. Again, you will often be moving about the text. You demonstrate how God's people successfully or unsuccessfully embraced the divine remedy for their spiritual sickness. This idea is applied to your congregation. In this way, your preaching idea becomes the reversal (the remedy) to the disequilibrium you have created (the spiritual sickness).

Last, you use the closing minutes to demonstrate the implications of accepting or rejecting this remedy. You show how acceptance brings spiritual health, while rejection brings further illness. You appeal to people to choose health (life) over disease (death).

Preaching this way enables you and your people to feel the story as drama. The sermon, which has its own plot, uses the pieces of the story that reflect the disequilibrium, reversal, and resolution they felt when they first read or heard the story. However, you have used the story as story, and the idea of the story has caused the congregation to wrestle with the disequilibrium of humanness, to understand and feel the reversal of divine truth, and choose the resolutions that provide life. Both the sermon and the text (a narrative) have been treated as story.

Conclusion

Preaching narratives is a delight. Finding the main idea of the story is a mysterious adventure that results in a wonderful climax. Leading a congregation through disequilibrium is also a grand adventure. Watching people go through an "aha" experience as the sermon plot is revealed is awesome. Finally, leading them to resolutions that are real, because they are based on true narratives, is genuinely satisfying. You will preach ideas you never thought the Bible articulated. And, as a result, you will see congregations make choices that are astounding.

Above all else, remember that the power in preaching comes from the Spirit's use of God's Word. You and I are instruments through which God often seeks to work.

For Further Reflection

Getting the Idea

1. What is this chapter talking about?
2. What is this chapter saying about what it's talking about?

Building on the Idea

1. Does the original language play a significant role in the exegesis of narrative?
2. How can the interpreter be sure that a narrative unit is a whole unit in and of itself?
3. How should sermons on narrative passages sound distinct?

Recommended Reading

Jensen, Richard A. *Telling the Story.* Minneapolis: Augsburg, 1980.

Larsen, David L. *Telling the Old, Old Story.* Wheaton: Crossway, 1995.

Lowry, Eugene L. *How to Preach a Parable: Designs for Narrative Sermons.* Nashville: Abingdon, 1989.

Miller, Calvin. "Narrative Preaching." In Michael Duduit, ed., *Handbook of Contemporary Preaching.* Nashville: Broadman, pp. 103–16.

Wiersbe, Warren. *Preaching and Teaching with Imagination: The Quest for Biblical Ministry.* Grand Rapids: Baker, 1994.

Preaching the Big Idea to Cultures and Subcultures

Exegeting the Culture

Terry Mattingly

> The expositor must also be aware of the currents swirling across his own times, for each generation develops out of its own history and culture and speaks its own language.[1]

The Baptist preacher had a mysterious look on his face as he gestured to me across a crowed hall at Denver Seminary. He spoke in a low voice. "Look, Mr. Mattingly," he asked. "What did *you* think of *Thelma & Louise*?"

I need to set the scene at this point. You see, this is a parable about how clergy end up on a different wavelength than the people who sit in the pews or who live in neighborhoods surrounding their churches. And it sheds light on one of the toughest tasks that Haddon Robinson has faced while teaching people how to preach.

It was the fall of 1991, a few months after I left my job as a religion reporter at the *Rocky Mountain News* to work with Haddon Robinson on a project attempting to integrate studies in popular culture and mass media into the seminary's core curriculum. On this particular day, I was the speaker at a luncheon for clergy, alumni, and others interested in the seminary and, in particular, its postgraduate studies.

I told them what I had been telling my students: that they live and minister in a culture built on language and symbols created by mass media. Modern media are so invasive and pervasive that church leaders simply cannot afford to ignore them.

Clergy can respond to this reality in one of two ways: (1) they can be so threatened by it that they remain silent; (2) they can learn to think like missionaries and use popular culture as a source of insights and information for ministry.

Popular culture is a warped mirror of our lives, but a mirror nonetheless. To use approach No. 1 is to be purely negative. Approach No. 2 mixes criticism of mass media's contents and social role with a sobering realization of the power that media have in modern life. It is realistic, critical, and, ultimately, constructive.

At one time or another, most of the people at that luncheon had heard Haddon Robinson say that they needed to exegete their culture as well as exegete the Word of God. That was bad enough. Now here was a journalist standing at a seminary podium telling them that they needed to try to pay critical attention to magazines and movies and television and talk shows and then take what they learned with them into the pulpit.

Many of the preachers were not amused and the discussion after my lecture was lively, to say the least. One pastor bluntly said that he couldn't get up in his pulpit and talk about movies, because that would mean admitting that he had *seen* them. Another added: "If I do that, I have a couple of deacons and big givers who will kill me."

We broke for lunch and that was when the Baptist preachers began pulling me aside. Three different pastors found a way to raise the same question: What did I think of *Thelma & Louise* (director Ridley Scott's explosive feminist manifesto that had been making headlines all summer). Eventually, actresses Susan Sarandon and Geena Davis ended up on the June 24, 1991 cover of *Time*, with the confrontational headline "Why *Thelma & Louise* Strikes a Nerve."

I gave the preachers an honest answer. I hadn't seen the movie. But I did have an entire file folder full of essays and reviews about the film. I was aware it had served as the latest spark igniting the gasoline of our culture's ongoing debates over sex roles. I was planning to wait and see if the movie would have a lasting impact. Then I would rent it on videocassette and, with pen and notepad in hand, sit down in a responsible and controlled environment—perhaps with seminary colleagues—and take careful notes.

But clearly, I needed to turn this question around. I didn't have a pulpit. They did. They were pastors, with the responsibility of guiding pilgrims in the modern world. They were experienced preachers. Plus, it was these preachers—not me—who had on this occasion ventured into the risky environment of a multiplex sanctuary.

By the time the third preacher cornered me, I was ready to ask the questions that needed to be answered: What did *he* think of *Thelma & Louise*? Why had *he* chosen to go see it?

Well, yes, he saw the *Time* cover. And, yes, he had heard about the movie from his wife, who heard some of her friends talking about it. And then he overheard a conversation in the church office. He knew that some women in the church had seen the movie and were still talking about it. His instincts told him this was something worth pursuing.

So far, so good, I said. What nerve did he think the movie struck?

Now he was on uncertain ground. Clearly, he said, it had something to do with female anger.

Okay, I asked. What were Thelma and Louise angry about?

Well, he said, husbands and lovers had abused them, or abandoned them, or both. Other men tricked them, or attacked them, or failed to make or honor commitments. Even good men who were sympathetic managed, in subtle ways, to keep a safe distance. Thelma and Louise felt stranded. Then they got mad. Then they tried to get even.

This is very interesting, I said. Why did he think this message appealed to more than a few women in his conservative Christian flock? Why were they forming packs, or slipping off solo, to

83

sit in the dark and watch this movie? And, come to think of it, did he have any angry women in his church?

Now he was very uncomfortable. Sure, he said, some women in his church were angry for some of the same reasons. His congregation contained its share of divorces and some had been messy. There was emotional abuse and one or two cases of physical abuse. A few husbands had vanished and there were times when he wished some other men would take a hike, too. Behind the scenes, many wives complained that their husbands were workaholics and emotionally distant. Some of them felt like single moms.

Yes, he said, there were angry and grieving women in his church.

Are some of them, I asked, the women who were going to see *Thelma & Louise*?

He nodded—yes.

Well, to me this sounded like this might be worth a sermon.

Yes, it did, the pastor said. But he knew that there was no way he could preach it. For one thing, he wasn't sure he could afford to preach about such an emotional, volatile topic. He also knew that many in his congregation would be upset if he quoted an R-rated movie, let alone suggested that it raised questions relevant to the church. Even some who had seen *Thelma & Louise,* and identified with it, might be upset if their pastor said that the film asked valid questions, but offered dangerous answers.

It would just be too risky. He could go and see the movie, but he couldn't admit that he had done so. The insights and feelings inspired by the movie couldn't be applied, at least directly, to the lives of his people. He was caught in a painful dilemma, a wrenching separation of church and life. Trouble was, this signal was coming from a sector of life that his church had declared out of bounds.

I asked one final question. So, his people went to the mall and the movie multiplex to find sermons on these kinds of life-wrenching issues?

Once again he nodded—yes.

Speaking to the Questions of the Age

> Men or women who speak effectively for God must first struggle
> with the questions of their age and then speak to those questions
> from the eternal truth of God. . . . To expound the Scriptures so
> the contemporary God confronts us where we live requires the
> preacher study his audience as well as his Bible.[2]

Day after day, our culture sends us signals.

Many, if not most, are worthless. Thus, we have a tendency to
ignore them. This is especially true of visual media—especially
television. Television is everywhere, so we no longer notice many
of its messages. As media researcher Neil Postman has noted:
"Television has become . . . the background radiation of the social
and intellectual universe, the all-but-imperceptible residue of the
electronic big bang of a century past, so familiar and so thoroughly integrated with American culture that we no longer hear
its faint hissing in the background or see the flickering gray
light."[3]

Some people have a gift for sorting through the static and seeing the patterns, hearing the signals and then figuring out a way
to deliver a response. This doesn't mean that this work is easy.
This doesn't mean that anyone has found a perfect way to teach
others how to perform these kinds of intellectual and spiritual
gymnastics. But somewhere in the middle of his ministry, Haddon Robinson began urging his students to try to take the leap.
Perhaps this had something to do with the lessons he learned
studying communication at the University of Illinois at Urbana-
Champaign, where he used an early computer the size of a ware-
house to help pinpoint patterns in his data on religious broad-
casting.

"Most of you cannot conceive of a world without television
and television has come to dominate the life of men and women
throughout the world as books did three and four hundred years
ago," said Robinson, in a 1991 Denver sermon ranging from oral
tradition and clay-tablet libraries to satellites and computer net-
works. "Television is omnipresent. We have now moved in our
society into a postliterate society. The way in which people get

85

ideas, the way in which they shape their ideals, comes not because they read books, but because they see it, they visualize it. It's on television."[4]

Most church leaders have been taught how to work and preach in the culture of books. They feel comfortable with books. They know how to respond, in the pulpit, to most concepts that they encounter in print. They are less comfortable with the barrage of images, concepts, and feelings that they encounter at the multiplex in the mall, in lobbies and waiting rooms, at the local video-rental establishments, or on the TV screens strategically located in their own homes and those of their parishioners.

If asked to do so, most seminary-educated pastors could write a paper or preach a sermon about why it is important to believe that the Word of God contains absolute truths that can help people make tough decisions in daily life. Many pastors would be able to debate a representative of another world religion, drawing lines between its beliefs and centuries of Christian teaching. But it's highly likely that those same preachers would struggle— or be totally lost—if shown episodes of Oprah in which she winsomely tells story after tear-jerking story about how people follow the whispers in their hearts and then find happiness and wholeness. In other words, truth is rooted in human experience and there are few, if any, moral absolutes.

These pastors may have been required to take a seminary course that would help them debate a Hindu believer. But no one told them that screenwriters and producers would take the same concepts and, backed with multimillion-dollar budgets, beam them into living rooms in the form of mesmerizing myths and parables. Odds are that their apologetics professor didn't apply the Bible to "Star Trek" and its "Prime Directive."

We live in an age of visual sermons. We are entertained by them, but do not take them seriously. Above all, we do not understand that *how* visual media communicate is just as important as *what* they communicate. We soak up the symbols and stories, while waiting for the secular media's principalities and powers to send us a book containing propositions we can refute with logical, linear arguments based on chapter and verse. Look at advertising. One of the few things on which most Americans agree is that they are not influenced by advertisements. Yet most people walking in the mall can sing dozens of jingles, fill in the blanks in hundreds of ad slogans, and their likes and dislikes have, in large part, been shaped by years of images—a video catechism of what it means to be alive.

But few ads today make their pitch using lines of type and linear arguments. Instead, they show us images. Some are funny and some are stupid, but they are almost always colorful and gripping. Truth is, these images are the first step in a kind of sacramental system. Step 1: See this image, experience this feeling, feel this need. Step 2: Buy and consume this product. Step 3: Accept, by faith, that using or consuming this product will help you become like the people in the images. The goal is to be able to say, "I am the kind of person who consumes this product." Whether they realize it or not, millions of people make professions of faith at the shopping mall.

This behavior transcends logic. Media theorists Luigi and Allesandra Maclean Manca note that "consumers tend to act toward a product as if it had a soul or a personality of its own. The function of advertising is therefore to suggest or even create this soul in the minds of the consumers. . . . This is obviously a pseudo-spirituality. Viewing the crime, fear, organized violence, poverty, racism, and genocide that are also part of our daily lives, it seems likely that we actually have a great spiritual void."[5]

Visual images are especially effective at telling stories and stirring emotions. They paint in broad, symbolic strokes, with the images building in layers, shaping opinions and attitudes.

"We are in an antagonistic environment," Robinson said, in that 1991 sermon. "It's an environment that communicates with images. It doesn't come out and argue. It just simply shows you pictures—day after day after day after day. Before you realize it, in the basement of your mind, you discover that you have shifted your values and many times you've lost your faith. That's a change. . . . When you watch television, people are robbed and raped and murdered and they never pray. They never seek out a minister. They never bother going to church. That world of television is a world in which God has no place. It's the world we live in." If the church doesn't take this change seriously, he noted, then "we are going to be left in the exhaust fumes of the society."

"Few church leaders will come right out and say that the church should ignore these changes," said Robinson. But when challenged to address the symbols and sermons in popular culture most preachers respond with silence. They have not been taught how to respond. Often, they have been taught that they should not attempt to do so.

Taking Advantage of Insights

> In quoting the Greek poets and philosophers, of course, Paul was not endorsing Athenian philosophy to Athenian philosophers. . . . In quoting the pagan sources, Paul merely took advantage of insights consistent with biblical revelation and more easily accepted by his hearers.[6]

The Master of Divinity student was confused and angry. Why was it so important, he asked, to analyze news and entertainment trends? Everyone knows that the secular media are liberal and opposed to the church. So why spend so much classroom time talking about popular culture? After all, he said, he came to seminary to learn how to be a pastor. What did this media stuff have to do with that?

"Now, pretend that I don't speak fluent evangelical," I said. "Tell me, in simple English, about a subject that really matters to seminary students."

In the front row, one student answered: "Discipleship."

That's a code word, I said. What does "discipleship" mean?

The student said that he wanted his ministry to touch the real lives of real people. He wanted to affect their views on the big issues, such as jobs, marriage, and money. "I want the faith to affect . . . how they really live," he said.

I agreed. Discipleship, if taken seriously, should have an impact on checkbooks, pocket calendars, parenting, and daily life. Then I pivoted and pointed to my list of the major forms of modern mass media—television, advertising, movies, print and video news media, popular music, and so on. Of course, these secular media, I joked, don't influence how people view work, success, sex, family, divorce, children, life, death, or eternity. And the people who run the media never ignore or knock Christianity. Right?

Looking around, I could see lights clicking on. At that moment, I improvised a kind of journalistic definition of "discipleship," consisting of three questions: How do you spend your time? How do you spend your money? How do you make your decisions? If pastors can answer these questions today in America without colliding with the power of mass media, then they have a promising future in ministry to the Amish.

Yes, this is a secular, highly statistical definition.[7] But asking and answering these kinds of practical questions will force church leaders to study the lives of the people they want to reach. Again and again, Haddon Robinson reminds speakers that they must try to understand what is inside the heads and hearts of those to whom they speak.

When it comes to these kinds of issues, any missionary who came to North America would quickly grasp the pivotal role mass media play in this culture. Often, Americans cannot see this because the subject is too big. It is like the old Chinese proverb about the fish that, when asked to describe its life, forgot to mention water.

How can preachers learn to think more like missionaries? Every time Paul entered a new land he seems to have headed straight to the synagogue and the marketplace. Any preacher who wants to do this today will need to study the signals that people receive while sitting on their couches or strolling through their malls.

So what is a "signal"? I define this as a single piece of media or popular culture focusing on a subject that is of vital interest to the church. It can be a newspaper article, a single episode of a television show, a compact disc, a movie, a new video, a best-selling book, or some other item. The goal is to tune in a single worthy signal, out of the millions the media pour over us every day. Above all, preachers must learn to recognize when the media launch a major invasion into biblical territory.

In the *Thelma & Louise* case, those preachers had found a solid signal. How? They spotted evidence in other media that this was an important film. This kind of crossover effect is common. For example, newspapers usually write advance stories about controversial movies or television programs. Also, these preachers listened to members of their families and congregations. It is crucial for preachers to find some forum in which they can talk to the unchurched. Youth ministers can ask young people to provide news clippings about their favorite artists or videos by their favorite bands. Above all, church leaders must listen and pay attention. I have never stood in a packed church lobby and failed to overhear people talking about movies or television shows. Once again: think like a missionary.

Getting the Signals Right

Most signals fall into three categories. The first is a signal that is so obvious that even the secular media recognize that it has moral and theological content. These signals reach a very high percentage of the population, in and out of the pews. The movie version of *The Silence of the Lambs* put the subject of evil and sin on the cover of *Time* and a preacher that read the novel would have found a revealing study of theodicy. Every year or two, the culture rides another wave of interest in life-after-death and near-death experiences. A list of such obvious topics would go on and on.

The second signal can be seen as a rifle shot at a specific niche in the population. Anyone who works with single adults knows that their media lives are different from those of adults who are married or who have children. Today, youth workers must ask *which* youth culture is most relevant. But they can never forget that cable television and satellites have wiped away many regional differences. Members of a youth group in the Appalachian hills may have been just as devastated by the 1994 suicide of grunge rocker Kurt Cobain as teens in big-city suburbs.

This is one of the most frustrating aspects of mass media to most church leaders. The same media that create national trends and myths also carve congregations into tiny camps of people who speak different languages. One day, the young people are talking about aliens and the paranormal. The next day, it's on "60 Minutes" or "The Today Show" and grandparents are asking for guidance. Preachers fear that, by addressing a signal that hits one part of the congregation, they will alienate everyone else. There is no one spirit of the age—they are legion. But the solution to this problem isn't silence. Here is the general rule: the broader the audience touched by a signal, the more likely it can be used effectively in the pulpit. If the niche is small, then this issue should be addressed in smaller forums, such as retreats or seminars.

Finally, there are signals that are important precisely *because* they haven't exploded into the public consciousness—yet. Often, it is possible to hear whispers in the popular culture about issues that will soon be shouted from the rooftops. This is where church leaders must concede that screenwriters, musicians, and journalists often do a better job of monitoring the public pulse than do religious educators, entrepreneurs, and bureaucrats.

Musician and writer John Fischer has noted: "No one can paint a picture of being lost better than someone who is lost and cannot see the way. . . . In many ways, the world is its own best critic. The keenest indictments against the world come from the pages of its journalists, commentators, artists, and comics. The funny pages of a newspaper can convey the most scathing of social criticism, showing how the world's attempts to solve its own problems often come up short.[8]"

Preachers may fear that they will wander through the pop-culture fields, picking through mass media haystacks in search for the right illustration to plug into one of their sermon outlines. They're right. That would be a tremendous waste of time. Instead, they should listen to their own people as they describe the truths and lies they encounter in popular culture. Once again:

How do they spend their time? How do they spend their money? How do they make their decisions?

From the Mall to the Pulpit

So a preacher finds a worthy signal. Now what? While working with Haddon Robinson, I developed a four-step process to get from the mall to the pulpit.

Step 1, obviously, is to find a specific media signal, as previously defined.

Step 2 requires honest, open-minded analysis. We want to find what I call the signal's "secular subject," as the artist would define it. Interviews often contain clues. Remember that artists must attract and hold an audience. In one way or another they have to deal with real issues or with what we could even call "big ideas"—life, death, love, hate, money, marriage, sex, fear, children, anger, pride, hatred, war, and so forth. We must ask: What was the subject that the artist wanted to address?

Step 3 mirrors step 2. Once you have found this "secular subject," it will almost always have moral or theological overtones. It will be a "sacred subject" that we share in common with the saints and sinners down through the ages. Stories change. Images change. Questions often sound new and strange. But the "big ideas" are remarkably constant, because the stuff of human experience is the same. Doctrines exist and the Bible is relevant to each generation because the "sacred subjects" don't change. At this point, seminary-educated pastors and other church leaders are within shouting distance of the media-dominated lives of millions of Americans.

Step 4 is the hardest part, because it requires church leaders to think of ways to respond. This does not require a television network or digital equipment. The church must respond by using its strengths—preaching, Christian education, prayer groups, retreats, and other traditional forms of ministry.

However, it is crucial actually to quote media signals as part of a response. In other words, the myths and messages we consume on our couches and at our malls matter. We must talk to our people about their real lives and, like it or not, this means talking about popular culture. We must admit that we are listening. We must try to understand.

By doing so, we are not letting the world hijack the church's agenda. We will merely be taking part in a debate in which the church cannot afford to remain silent. We cannot do so without studying signals from popular culture and then openly discussing them in the church.

Preachers who dare to do this will find that people will discuss these subjects—a lot. They will not be dispassionate. They will challenge opinions and criticize judgments. They will bend the preacher's ear. They will ask questions. Many will ask for help.

For many church leaders these reactions will be frightening, at first. But this is a reason to address media issues, not a reason to turn and run. We must admit that most of our people do not have the media under control. If anything, it is the other way around.

It would be easy to get depressed. It would be easy to be discouraged and to say that this task is impossible, that it will require a kind of honesty that is impossible in our churches. Others will say that the church is already too far behind, so it is better not even to try to defend timeless truths from those who attack them in the modern age.

Haddon Robinson knows all of that. But he still believes that God can use preaching to shed light in our time, in this age. If churches and seminaries will not do what needs to be done, "then God will go on and do other things," he said, as he concluded his sermon that day in Denver. "We always live in the light of his triumph. He doesn't need us. He doesn't need folks who are sure that they are going to do it the way they've always done it. He passes by churches. He blows out lamps. He moves on to other things. The only question is whether we are going to move with Him, or stay where we are and let the fire fall someplace else. That is the challenge and if we do not rise to it, someone else will. God's work will be done—with us or without us."

For Further Reflection

Getting the Idea

1. What is this chapter talking about?
2. What is this chapter saying about what it's talking about?

Building on the Idea

1. Why is it important for the preacher to understand culture?
2. What are the characteristics of "media signals" for the preacher in the preparation of sermons?
3. What are some of the issues you face as you attempt to exegete culture? In what way would you take advantage of Mattingly's suggestions to address these issues?

Recommended Reading

Brown, Steve, Robinson, Haddon, and William Willimon. *A Voice in the Wilderness: Clear Preaching in a Complicated World.* Sisters, Oreg.: Multnomah, 1993.

Duduit, Michael, ed. *Communicate with Power: Insights from America's Top Communicators.* Grand Rapids: Baker, 1996.

Hull, William E. "The Contemporary World and the Preaching Task." In Michael Duduit, ed., *Handbook of Contemporary Preaching.* Nashville: Broadman, 1992, pp. 571–87.

Hybels, Bill, Briscoe, Stuart, and Haddon Robinson. *Mastering Contemporary Preaching.* Portland: Multnomah, 1990.

Miller, Calvin. *Marketplace Preaching: How to Return the Sermon to Where It Belongs.* Grand Rapids: Baker, 1995.

The Big Idea and Biblical Theology's Grand Theme

Bruce L. Shelley

In the Bible patriarchs, prophets, and disciples enter the story, play their parts, and then exit left or right before a landscape of unimaginable grandeur. Their personal lives find meaning only in the light and shadows of eternity. The curtain rises on creation, then scenes of Moriah, Exodus, Sinai, Bethlehem, and Calvary pass only to fade—without ending—into "the life to come."

Preaching masters tell us that the message in this saga gives birth to theology. And theology in turn, when it is full grown, delivers preaching from the chains of boredom and triviality. At least that is the story I get from the preaching masters. Fred Craddock, for example, once said, "Small topics are like pennies; even when polished to a high gloss, they are still pennies." It is theology alone that dares to ask the preacher, "What ultimate vision are you holding before us?"[1]

This much is certain: preaching and theology are united for life. There is a theology for preaching; and there is a theology of preaching. What you think about preaching heavily influences how you preach. It is as simple as that.

Haddon Robinson spent forty years teaching students how to preach. But students had to listen carefully to catch from him what preaching is. Obviously, "the father of big idea preaching" had his own idea of what "preaching" means, but his book *Biblical Preaching* itself is all about the preparation and delivery of sermons.

During the twelve years that we worked together closely, I probably heard Haddon Robinson preach scores of times. During the same years he also profoundly influenced my two sons in his classes. I think I got to know the man rather well. After looking back upon the years, I would describe Haddon Robinson as a "realist."

As president of our seminary, he wasn't sure how to handle "pietists," those people in every Christian organization who respond to life emotionally. He was a man who taught his students "how to make good decisions." And if we recall that he grew up in New York City, we might even call him "street smart."

No surprise, then, that the legacy he leaves to thousands of preachers is a book about "how to transform your ministry." I gladly confess he changed mine. His influence on my life came late in my career—after speech classes, hermeneutics, homiletics, and twenty years of preaching. So the influence was not primarily informational. I'd call it inspirational. Yet it changed completely the way I thought about the preaching task and how I prepared for it. Old dogs can learn new tricks!

The Really Big Idea

My purpose here, however, is something more than singing the praises of an outstanding preacher. I'd like to take Robinson's approach so seriously as to engage it at some vital point and the most vital point I know springs from his stress on the development of the exegetical "big idea."

I want to ask here, "Is there a big idea in the Bible itself? A big idea beyond all big ideas in the various passages a preacher might choose for a text?" And if there is, then shouldn't this big idea or grand theme color every homiletical idea we preach?

Here, in a single declarative sentence, is my point: The big idea of an expository sermon should be developed as a personal truth.

The conviction of the "should" hit me not long ago while reading Walter Burghardt's helpful volume, *Preaching: The Art and the Craft.* At one point he recalls his early days of preaching to Catholic congregations. "When I began to preach four decades ago," he writes, "the Catholic stress was on the clear and distinct idea. Our seminary education, in philosophy and theology, emphasized objectivity. We were the dispassionate searchers for the truth, cool critics of error and heresy—beetle-browed, lynx-eyed, hard-nosed, square-jawed. Imagination was for poets. We did not show our emotions. Emotions were for women."[2]

While reading these words I recalled how many young Protestant preachers just out of seminary I had heard and how often they tended to explain the meaning of some word or some insight from the original text. On occasion they also seemed bound by some technique of delivery. While preaching the Word of Truth the thoughts in their heads often dulled the passions in their hearts.

This fever in the brain, I discovered, is especially acute in pastors who neglect their people. After more than thirty years of preaching it kindled my memory and I said to myself, "If I had only listened to my people more, I know I would have come to terms with human emotions more quickly and thus to the feelings in the passage."

The young preachers that I had in mind were seldom products of Haddon Robinson's classes. With his stress on images, stories, and plot I know that emotionless sermons were never part of the master's method.

Still this problem I had with some preaching raised the question in my mind, "Why must the big idea drawn from a passage of Scripture only be developed in four ways?" That, as I recalled, is what Robinson said: "The preacher can restate it, explain it, prove it, and apply it. That's all!"

Feeling the Truth

I want to propose here, respectfully I trust, a fifth way. We can also feel the big idea. But hear me out. I'm talking here about a special feeling related to the Grand Theme itself.

I believe firmly that propositional truth matters. Truth about God matters supremely. I join many evangelical Christians in the belief that if we think the wrong thing about God it will not be long before we start feeling and doing the wrong thing as well.

But I also believe that doctrine and propositional truth are not enough if the heart is cold and the will unmoved. The truth we preach must be a truth not just thought, but also felt and done.

I think Haddon Robinson assumes this fifth way of developing a big idea but I haven't been able to find the explicit suggestion anywhere in *Biblical Preaching*. It is possible, I suppose, to detect the feeling element when he stresses the application of the big idea. The significance of feelings may also lie hidden in his emphasis on discovering the meaning of the passage in the author's intent. But I want to ask, "What about the overriding intent of God? How does he make his appeal through us?"

If, as Haddon Robinson says, we are to preach the flow of thought, what about the flow of feeling? Isn't there a subjective element in the biblical revelation accompanying the cognitive or rational element? And don't most young or inexperienced preachers need to develop that "pietistic" element too?

If they want to be heard, it seems to me, they have to come to terms with the feeling within the passage, because the big idea in preaching—if it is true—is always more than an idea.

The thought within the text always has a texture. "Words, woven into the fabric of meaning," Eugene Peterson writes, "have a characteristic *feel* to them." When our fingers touch a textile we know what the fabric is good for—silk for ribbons, denim for jeans, wool for sweaters. So with preaching. "Getting the feel of the text is prerequisite to getting its meaning."[3]

The preaching masters develop this touch. In one of his famous lectures to Yale students Phillips Brooks observed: "Much of our preaching is like delivering lectures upon medicine to sick people. The lecture is true. The lecture is interesting. Nay, the truth of the lecture is important, and if the sick man could learn the truth of the lecture he would be a better patient, he would take his medicine more responsibly and regulate his diet more intelligently. But still the fact remains that the lecture is not medicine, and that to give the medicine, not to deliver the lecture, is the preacher's duty."[4]

The "medicine," I take it, is the gospel, the truth of God's Word. Brooks saw clearly that truth in the biblical sense of the word is not merely, or even primarily, a child of the intellect. It is basically a characteristic of persons. The Hebrew word for truth [emeth] means "trustworthy," "faithful," or "reliable." And Jesus, we should recall, spoke of "doing the truth" and "being the truth."[5]

To this day the personal meaning of truth and the whole-person meaning of "heart" survive in English usage whenever we speak of "a true friend" or of a married couple being "true to each another." If I am true to someone, that is more than treasuring lovely thoughts about her or him.

This little fact from the Bible throws a floodlight on the meaning of biblical preaching. Far too often we slip into the assumption of our Western culture that truth is primarily a matter of the mind. We assume that if people think the right things, then feeling and doing the right things will naturally follow.

But the Bible does not separate the intellect from the emotions and the will that way. The special kind of truth we find in the Bible is a blended truth in which intellectual assent, emotional involvement, and volitional commitment interpenetrate each other when we wholeheartedly embrace the Christian faith. Biblical truth is a function not just of propositions but of persons—supremely of God.

Biblical preaching, to borrow Ian Pitt-Watson's image, is like taking off in a Boeing 727. To soar you need all three engines of faith: intellect, emotion, and will. Ultimately, God, far more than the preacher, is the communicator. In the preacher's words, God is communicating himself. In his divine foolishness he speaks through our fumblings and bumblings in the pulpit, and on occasion—thanks to his grace—even in spite of them.[6]

The Grand Theme

Another reason to develop the personal element of the big idea lies in the fact that the preacher's sermonic idea should be related to biblical theology's grand theme.

Since the days of the apostles, preaching and Christ have been intimately linked. He is more than the message we preach. He is the reason we preach and the reward of all our efforts. Through the centuries preachers like Calvin, Augustine, and Brooks, men who dared to tell others how to preach, have recognized a persistent theme that runs like a gold and scarlet thread through the Bible. Some called it "the knowledge of God," "the covenant," or "redemption's story."

The most persistent phrase is probably "the Word of God." Pastors, preachers, and reformers, like Luther, recognized that this dominant theme comes to us in three ways: first, in Jesus Christ, the Word made flesh; second, in the written Word of Scripture; and third—as amazing as grace itself!—in the Word preached!

But only in the twentieth century have scholars identified the grand theme and traced the development of its various strands from Genesis to Revelation. This is what we call "biblical theology."

And how preachers need it when they find themselves, like Phillips Brooks, praying for deliverance from trivial preaching! During the course of his famous lectures over a century ago, Brooks urged his audience to take up their Saturday newspapers and check the list of titles that the ministers of any great city were announcing for their sermons the next day. You can readily detect, he said, what small and fantastic bits of truth congregations are getting from their preachers.

You will find there, Brooks insisted, striking evidence of the little preaching coming from little pulpits. "The quality our preaching most lacks is breadth. I mean largeness of movement, the great utterance of great truths, as distinct from the minute and ingenious treatment of side issues of the soul's life, the bric-a-brac of theology."[7]

Today, under the pressure of popularity and the stress of weekly sermon preparations, how many of us struggle to come up with some big idea from the passage, only to settle for bric-a-brac?

Often we think biblical preaching means sprinkling an assortment of scriptural texts throughout the sermon. But frequent quotation of Scripture is no reliable index of the biblical authenticity of a sermon. Too often texts are mere pretexts for the grand theme. Our most direct step toward a significant big idea from a given passage of Scripture is to search for the passage's link with the grand theme.

Preaching drawn from the grand theme is also more than preaching "doctrine" in the usual sense of the term. "The truth is," Brooks affirmed, "no preaching ever had any strong power that was not the preaching of doctrine . . . No exhortation to a good life that does not put behind it some truth as deep as eternity can seize and hold the conscience. Preach doctrine, . . . but preach it always, not that men may believe it, but that men may be saved by believing it."[8]

This is what I mean by preaching related to the grand theme and preaching with a personal tone. Here lies the reason Pitt-Watson says in his *Primer for Preachers* "biblical theology *belongs* to preachers." It can never be merely reflective or academic. It is at heart practical and personal. It came originally through preachers. Think of what the prophets did. Consider what the apostles are doing in the book of Acts. They seize the stream of historical redemptive events and bring them before an audience for decision. They issue a summons to appear before God because God wants a reply.

It is this meaning of truth and this understanding of biblical theology that leads me to conclude that preachers must develop their big idea while pondering feelings within the passage and the sermon.

The fact is ordinary people listen for a preacher's feelings as much as his ideas, perhaps more. That is simply part of the power of the spoken word. It not only makes something intelligible; it also reveals the character of the speaker. A preacher's tone, inflections, and force are all signs pointing into the hidden realms of character. Whatever excites or depresses a preacher usually reveals a small but significant bit of character.

There is a down side to this truth. Many people in our time have questions tucked away in their inner thoughts. They have developed a sensitivity toward speakers with a "know-it-all" or officious tone. They are quick to dump them in a class with "used car salesmen" or "politicians."

In North America today people tend to listen for compassion and understanding; they are eager to listen to those who "have been there"—where they are. So preaching cannot afford to be forced or faked; it cannot be imported from without. Preaching must be "me."

But if I preach, who am I? A modest study of preaching in New Testament times will reveal two important aspects of a preacher's task. The two are embodied in two words. One is message; the other is witness. Just two examples will suffice. In his first epistle John writes: "This is the message we have heard of him and declare to you." And in his words before the Jerusalem Council, Peter said: "We are his witnesses of these things."

That sums it up. So if I am a biblical preacher, I am a messenger and a witness. And my emotions ought to reflect both.

The Great Risk

There is a great risk, I know, in what I am saying. Feelings are a fragile and frail guide to the truth. They probably mislead as often as they lead to the truth. We know how often in the past preachers have exploited emotions to generate some religious experience or to rally support for some misdirected cause. This sort of misuse of emotion has given "rhetoric" the negative reputation it often carries today. Self-indulgent emotionalism in preaching has been as popular as theological error.

Felt truth alone is not enough. It must be reinforced by rigorous thinking and validated in Christian action. The truth we preach must be a truth not just felt, but also thought and done. But I still insist it must be felt.

At the heart of feelings inspired by the grand theme is gratitude for the grace of God. The wonder we feel when we realize that the Lord of heaven and earth has included us in his eternal plan seems to inspire a cluster of feelings or—as Jonathan Edwards called them—"religious affections." I mean affections like loyalty, devotion and fidelity, all traceable to God's grace, all demonstrable through our thoughts and actions.

The best illustration of the feeling of grace I know comes from Pitt-Watson's *Primer for Preachers*. In his last chapter he recalls an experience from his youth.

Some time around World War II, when young Ian was about fourteen, he came reluctantly to the conclusion that he just had to learn to dance. He didn't like the idea, but he saw his friends who were good dancers enjoying "certain social fringe benefits" that he was missing. So he decided that before making a public exhibition of his awkwardness he would master the art secretly and in private.

He bought himself a book called *Teach Yourself to Dance*. It contained detailed instructions and elaborate diagrams showing exactly what to do and where to put your feet. In this way Pitt-Watson testifies he mastered ballroom dancing 1930s style. He really knew the book and spent hours trying to put its diagrams into practice. He did so alone in his bedroom, using a pillow for a partner and studying his progress in the wardrobe mirror.

What he saw in the mirror was not reassuring! He was putting his feet in all the right places, doing what the book said. But something clearly was missing. He was thinking the right things and doing the right things, but he couldn't get the feel of it, and as a consequence everything he did seemed clumsy—graceless.

Then one night at a party a nice girl who knew of his difficulty said, "Come on, try it with me." So he did. To begin with he felt even more of a fool because he was so awkward and she was so full of grace. Then something strange happened. A little of her grace seemed to pass to him and he began to get the feel of it.

For the first time all he had learned in the book began to make sense, and even the painful practice in front of the mirror began to pay off. What had been contrived now became natural because at last he had got together what he was thinking, what he was feeling, and what he was doing. In that moment he experienced a kind of grace, and, as he says, it was beautiful![9]

True, preachers deal with another and much greater kind of grace. But it too comes to us when we get together truth thought, truth done, and truth felt. I am inclined to think this is the reason the Puritans made so much of "preparation of the heart" in their discussions of preaching. Consider the best example from Puritan preaching I know, the Puritan classic *Pilgrim's Progress*.

In Bunyan's classic story of Christian's journey from the City of Destruction to the Celestial City, he portrays Christian following the instructions of a man named Good-will; and he came in the course of his journey to the house of Interpreter. He knocked at the door, met the master of the house, and was ushered into a room, where he found something "profitable" for his journey:

> Christian saw the picture of a grave person hung up against the wall. It had eyes lifted up to heaven, the best of books in his hand, the law of truth was written on his lips, the world was behind his back; it stood as if it pleaded with men, and a crown of gold did hang over its head. "I have showed you this picture," Interpreter said, "because the man whose picture this is, is the only man whom the Lord of the place where you are going has authorized to be the guide in all difficult places."

What Shall We Do?

Before such an image of preaching, what does it take to preach personally?

Let's start in the study. Preachers ought to develop the big idea of their sermon while considering how their people hear them. The preacher's constant question must be: How does my congregation hear these words? As I recall, it was the highly respected theologian John Courtney Murray who once remarked, "I do not know what I have said until I understand what you have heard." A truly biblical message lays on the preacher a double demand: I must say what I mean, but I must also sense what my people hear.

Second, if the preacher is to sense what his people hear, he must look for the Word in human experience. The Scriptures, we know, throw a revealing light on human experiences, but are we also aware how much the text of life can illuminate a passage of Scripture?

Jesus preached like an artist paints. A master painter can take a bit of chalk or a burnt stick and create a human face that will make you laugh, or weep, or wonder. Jesus used words in the same way. He took common life around him—children playing in the marketplace or at a funeral, the sewing of a piece of cloth onto an old garment, or the crumbling of a hut in a storm—and he created striking pictures of a higher life. No wonder the crowds followed him!

So many of the great truths of the Bible are pictured in our daily human experiences. When a preacher reads these two texts together he creates a binocular vision that can see both realities as one without distorting either. That is the unique perspective of a biblical preacher.

Burghardt describes this perspective as "looking for the holes in the world or listening to the space between sounds. It is breaking through the obvious, the surface, the superficial, to the reality beneath and beyond."[10]

Third, the emotion in the sermon should reflect the emotion of the text. If that happens in our sermons we have to prepare our hearts for it just as we prepare our heads. This is the lesson from the Puritans, who believed that the preacher could capture not only the ideas of the passage but its emotion as well, and that it was the duty of the preacher in preparing to preach to tune his heart to the passage as well as capture its truths in his head.

Who is sufficient for these things? How can worshipers in our time possibly hear God speak over the cynical, multimedia din of modern life? Thomas Long of Princeton Theological Seminary, one of the best known preachers in America, says that television has reduced some preaching to "sound-bytes, imagistic bursts and episodic narratives," but this may only whet the appetite for live speech. "The most powerful form of communication," Long insists, "is still one human being standing up and speaking courageous truth."[11]

For Further Reflection

Getting the Idea

1. What is this chapter talking about?
2. What is this chapter saying about what it's talking about?

Building on the Idea

1. State biblical theology's grand theme in your own words.
2. Is it possible for the grand theme to penetrate every sermon?
3. How does the preacher help listeners feel an idea that is basically doctrinal instruction?

Recommended Reading

Adam, Peter. *Speaking God's Words: A Practical Theology of Expository Preaching*. Downers Grove: InterVarsity, 1998.

Kaiser, Walter C., Jr. *Towards an Exegetical Theology: Biblical Exegesis for Preaching and Teaching.* Grand Rapids: Baker, 1981.

Pitt-Watson, Ian. *A Primer for Preachers.* Grand Rapids: Baker, 1986.

Mohler, R. Albert, Jr. "A Theology of Preaching." In Michael Duduit, ed., *Handbook of Contemporary Preaching.* Nashville, Broadman, 1992, pp. 113–20.

Smalley, Gary, and John Trent. *The Language of Love.* Colorado Springs: Focus on the Family, 1991.

Part 3

Big Idea Preaching

Communicating the Point

8

Sticking to the Plot

The Developmental Flow of the Big Idea Sermon

Donald R. Sunukjian

Developing a Clear Flow

Having studied the chosen passage, outlined the author's thought, and formed the big idea, the speaker is ready to prepare the message for a contemporary audience. This message should be clear and easy to follow, while remaining faithful to the biblical author's progression of ideas.

To develop a clear flow to the message, the speaker must repeatedly choose between a "deductive" or "inductive" approach at different places in the message.

First, let's define these two basic approaches, and then see how they operate at three different levels in the message: (1) in the overall structure, (2) in the "preview" statements, and (3) in the individual outline movements.

In a "deductive" approach, the speaker states a complete idea (a subject and a complement), and then either explains, proves, or applies that complete idea. The speaker makes an assertion, a declarative sentence, and then develops that sentence.

In an "inductive" approach, the speaker asks a question, and then allows the subsequent materials to provide the answer. The speaker raises the subject, but the complement doesn't emerge until later in the message.

Development of Exodus 13:17–22

To see how these two basic approaches repeatedly show up at different levels in the message, let's illustrate from outlines on two passages of Scripture: Exodus 13:17–22 and James 4:1–6.

The first concern in Exodus 13:17–22 (as in any message) is to outline the text's flow of thought and to form the big idea. At this point in Exodus, Pharaoh has capitulated and about 3 to 4 million Israelites are preparing to leave Goshen, where they have been slaves for hundreds of years (Exod. 12:37–42). Their destination is Canaan, the "Promised Land," the home of their ancestors. They can reach this destination in six to eight days by following the nearby international trade route that runs in a straight northeasterly direction—along the Mediterranean coastline, through the Philistine territory, and into Canaan.

But, according to Exodus 13:17–18, God does not lead them along this straight route, even though it is shorter and quicker. Instead, God leads the people "around," toward the southern desert and the Red Sea. The text gives a reason for this longer route: if God took them on the straight route, they would never make their destination—they would face some military threat (either from the Philistines or from Egypt's divisions stationed along this invasion corridor), change their minds, and return to Egypt.

The text then notes two particular features of this march to the south: a coffin containing the bones of Joseph (13:19) and a cloud capable of guiding by day or night (13:20–22). The coffin, lifted daily and carried by strong men, is a visible reminder that, though they are heading south, their ultimate destination is Canaan. They will bury the bones of their ancestor in the land God promised, according to an oath made hundreds of years earlier (Gen. 50:24–26). The cloud, which comes into their national existence at this unique moment and remains until their travels are complete (Exod. 40:36–38), becomes their guide (Num. 9:15–23), their protection from Pharaoh's chariots (Exod. 14:19–20) and the desert heat (Ps. 105:39; cf. Isa. 4:5–6), and the palpable presence of God in their midst (Exod. 33:7–10; Num. 12:5; Ps. 99:6–7).

Putting these concepts in outline form, the flow of thought in Exodus 13:17–22 would be as follows:

   I. God purposefully takes Israel from one point to another by means of an indirect route.
  II. The reason for God's leading is that Israel would never make it on the straight-line path.
 III. As the Israelites embark on this uncharted journey, God encourages them in two ways.
     A. He gives them a visible reminder of his good intentions.
     B. He gives them a palpable sense of his presence.

As the speaker reflects on this content, the big idea begins to take shape: God leads Israel on an indirect route to get them safely to his promised destination, along the way providing continual reminders of his good intentions and a palpable sense of his presence. While focusing on the early part of this sentence, and considering how to form the big idea into its final, and hopefully memorable, homiletic form, the speaker suddenly thinks of a contradictory variation of the well-known geometric axiom: "The shortest distance between two points is a zigzag."

The speaker is now ready to put together the final sermon outline. As we look at this outline, we'll see how the concepts of "deduction" and "induction" enable the speaker to present the biblical material with clarity and relevance to the contemporary listener.

   Introduction
   1. Early in geometry we learned, "The shortest distance between two points is a straight line."

2. That may be true in geometry, but as you and I consider what God is doing in our lives, we wonder if God doesn't think, "The shortest distance between two points is a zigzag."

3. That is, we find ourselves at Point A, convinced that God intends to take us to Point B. We can visualize a short, straight-line path between these two points. But if God is really taking us to Point B, he must be on a zigzag path. (At this point the speaker would give several examples of how the listeners might be experiencing this: the absence of anticipated promotions in a company; the lack of expected growth in an entrepreneurial business; the unraveling of a romantic relationship that could lead from singleness to marriage, etc. In each example the speaker would contrast the expected sequence of a straight-line path with God's apparent movement in the opposite direction.)

4. Today, I want you to see that sometimes, with God, the shortest distance between two points is a zigzag (deductive statement of the big idea).

5. (Preview) I want you to see that sometimes God deliberately takes us on a zigzag path (deductive). I want you to see why he does this (inductive). And I want you to see the good encouragement he gives us along the way (inductive).

I. In order to see that God sometimes deliberately leads us on a zigzag path, we'll look at a time in Israel's history when God deliberately takes them on a zigzag path (deductive).
   A. They are at Point A—Goshen, where they have been slaves for hundreds of years. (Briefly review the plagues and Pharaoh's capitulation.)
   B. Their destiny is Point B—Canaan, the Land of Promise.
   C. The shortest distance between Point A and Point B is a straight-line route along the Mediterranean coast and through the Philistine territory.
   D. But we read in Exodus 13:17–18 that God does not lead them on this direct route, but instead takes them on a zigzag path in the opposite direction. (Read vv. 17–18.)

II. The reason God takes us on a zigzag is because there is something in the straight-line path that would prevent us from ever reaching our destination (deductive).

A. God knows that if he takes the Israel on the direct route they will never make it. (Read and explain v. 18).

B. God knows there is something in our straight-line path that would prevent us from safely arriving at his intended destination. (The speaker can return to the examples given in Introduction 3, suggesting possible obstacles that God is aware of—a hostile executive who would sandbag continuing advancement in the company; the damage an accelerated business expansion and sudden wealth would do to a young family; the need to heal some past emotional hurt before an engagement would last.)

III. Because we might become dismayed in the midst of the zig and the zags, God encourages us in two ways (inductive).

A. God gives us continual reminders of his good intentions (deductive).

1. As Israel embarks on an uncharted route, God uses a coffin to remind them of their ultimate destination. (Read and explain v. 19.)

2. In the midst of our zigs and zags, God will find some way to remind us of his good intentions. (The speaker returns again to the previous examples to suggest how someone's innocent comment might unknowingly touch on our Point B, and become God's reminder that he is still working good in our life.)

B. God gives us a palpable sense of his presence (deductive).

1. As Israel embarks on an uncharted path, a pillar of cloud and fire appears, which guides, protects, and accompanies them the length of their travels. (Read and explain vv. 20–22.)

2. In the midst of our zigs and zags, we will experience the guidance, protection, and nearness of our God.

In developing the outline, the speaker repeatedly chooses either a "deductive" or "inductive" approach at different levels in the message: (1) in the overall structure, (2) in the "preview" statements, and (3) in the development of individual outline movements.

The first choice (Introduction 4) is for a deductive approach to the overall structure. After opening materials designed to engage the listener and develop a need for the message, the speaker makes a complete, declarative statement of the big idea (Introduction 4). The central truth of the message is revealed at the start.

The advantage of an overall deductive structure is that the big idea emerges early and clearly. The listener knows from the very beginning what the Word of God will say that day.

The disadvantage of an overall deductive structure is that it may "give away all the cookies at the start"—the suspense, or tension, or movement toward a climax may be lessened. The listener's attention might diminish, with a "been there, heard that" response.

Because of this potential disadvantage, the overall deductive structure is most effective when the Big Idea, clearly stated, causes the listener to immediately have some questions about it. These questions will be along the lines of:

- "I just heard your central truth, and I have no idea what you're talking about. Can you explain what you mean?"
- "I just heard your central truth, and I don't buy it for a minute. Can you prove what you just said, or show me why it's true?"
- "I just heard your central truth, and I either don't see that it has any bearing on my life, or I don't know what to do with it. Can you give me some examples so I know what it looks like in real life?"

These questions in the mind of the listener provide the continuing tension, or suspense, or reason to keep listening. The listener hopes the message will answer some of them, and remains mentally engaged.

If the big idea does not generate any absorbing questions in the mind of the listener, an overall inductive structure would probably be a better choice. (This will be illustrated in the example from James 4:1–6.)

In the outline above, the statement of the big idea probably raises questions in the listener's mind along the lines of: "Is that really true—that God takes zigzag paths to get us somewhere? Why would God do that? Why not lead in a more 'efficient' manner? How do I know if God is doing that in my life? I don't seem to be getting where I thought, but I still feel God intends some particular Point B for me. How does this relate to my specific situation?"

The second place in the outline where deductive/inductive choices are made is in the "preview" statements (Introduction 5) which immediately follow the big idea. The purpose of a preview is to give the listener a "map" of what's ahead—the broad strokes or movements that will appear in the body of the message, the main hunks that will emerge as the message unfolds. A preview immensely helps the listener "organize" the material to come.

In the example above, there are three preview statements (Introduction 5), corresponding to the three main movements of the message. The first statement is deductive—it fully reveals the content of the first main point (I.). Since that content has already been developed in the introduction, there is no suspense about it. In essence, the preview statement says, "I intend to prove from the Bible that the statement I made in the introduction is true."

The second and third preview statements, however, are inductively stated—they ask questions that will be answered later in the message; they raise the subjects of coming main points, but do not reveal the complements. They say to the listener, "You will have to keep listening to the message to find out the answer to these things."

A preview can have any combination of deductive/inductive elements, regardless of which approach is being used in the overall structure. (The possible exception is an overall inductive structure followed by only deductive preview statements. The deductive previews would probably answer the inductive question raised in the introduction, and in effect create an overall deductive structure.)

For example, a deductive idea could be followed by three deductive preview statements—idea: "Count your days to make your days count" (Ps. 90); previews: "The Scripture will tell us that human life is brief and troubled because of sin (90:1–11), but that numbering our days will motivate us to righteous living (90:12), and that this righteous living will result in God's blessing instead of sin's trouble (90:13–17)."

Or, an overall deductive structure, with a big idea in the introduction, could be followed by three inductive previews—idea: "God works all things for good"; previews: "We'll see what this does not mean, we'll see what the 'good' is that God has in mind, and we'll see how he works all things toward it."

Likewise, an overall inductive structure, set up by a question in the introduction, could be followed by two inductive previews (see the James 4:1–6 example which follows), or by one deductive and one inductive—question: "How do we know when we have successfully persevered through a trial?" (James 1:12); previews: "We'll see first that trials are intended to make us mature and complete, and then we'll see how we know when that has happened."

The choice of deduction/induction at one level of the message does not necessarily determine the choices made at another level, as we see further by examining the third place in the message where a choice must be made—in the development of individual outline movements.

The decision of whether to develop an individual movement deductively or inductively is usually determined by the nature of its subpoints. If the subpoints are a "list," the inductive approach is almost always preferable. If the subpoints are a "progression," the deductive approach will be the clearest.

The subpoints are a "list" when the same key terms occur in each subpoint, and when the order of the subpoints is logically interchangeable.

For example, the third movement (III.) in the Exodus 13 message is developed inductively because the subpoints (IIIA. and IIIB.) are a list. The speaker in essence raises the question (III.), "What are the two ways God encourages us?" and the subpoints list the two ways. The subpoints have the same key terms ("he encourages us by giving us . . ."), and, though the text presents them in a particular order, they conceivably could be in the reverse order and remain just as clear.

When an outline movement implies a numerical "list," the speaker would do well to ask a question at the start of the movement, and then allow the subsequent subpoints to build the complete answer. This inductive approach will sustain greater interest than if the speaker announces both "encouragements" at the start. To say—"Because we might become dismayed in the midst of the zigs and the zags, God encourages with continual reminders of his good intentions and a palpable sense of his presence"—is to give away more than is necessary and to make the unfolding development anticlimactic.

Sometime the subpoints in a movement are a "progression"—an unfolding sequence in either a narrative story or a reasoning chain. The tip-off that such a progression or sequence is occurring is that the last subpoint is the only one that contains the same key assertion as the larger concept. In such situations, for clarity's sake, the speaker should choose a deductive development of that particular movement.

For example, a deductive development is clearer for the first movement (I.) in the message above, since the subpoints progress through a narrative sequence, and the assertion of the larger concept does not appear until the last subpoint. If the speaker had approached the movement inductively, asking the question "What does God do to Israel?" the initial subpoints would not seem to be answering the question and the listener would become confused in the long wait for an answer at the end.

The second movement is another example where a deductive approach is preferable. Though the movement is previewed inductively so as to sustain initial suspense (Introduction 5), its actual development in the message is done deductively (II. and IIA.) because the subpoints in the expanded outline are a logical sequence, a progressive chain of reasoning, and because the assertion of the main concept is not reached until the final subpoint:

> II. The reason God takes us on a zigzag is because there is something in the straight-line path that would prevent us from ever reaching our destination.
> A. God knows that if he takes Israel on the direct route, they will never make it.
> 1. The international trade route leads past Egyptian defenses and through hostile Philistine territory.
> 2. Such a route might involve situations of war.
> 3. Israel, a nation of slaves, is unprepared for war.
> 4. The fear of such encounters would make Israel regret ever leaving Egypt.
> 5. Preferring slavery rather than death, Israel might return to Egypt and never make it to their destination.

Speakers occasionally make the mistake of approaching a "progression" inductively. They ask a question, knowing in their own minds that the answer will eventually come. But they do not realize that the listener is hearing the following, and becoming confused:

> II. Why does God take us on zigzag paths?
> A. Why does he take Israel on a zigzag path?
> 1. The international trade route leads past Egyptian defenses and through hostile Philistine territory.
> 2. Such a route might involve situations of war.
> 3. Israel, a nation of slaves, is unprepared for war.

After several minutes of such development, the listener still has not heard the answer, and may even have forgotten the question! When a movement's subpoints are a sequence or progression, the deductive approach is preferable.

Development of James 4:1–6

A second message, from James 4:1–6, illustrates the same deductive/inductive choices being made at different levels in the message. The particular choices are different, but the speaker is guided by the same considerations of interest and clarity.

The message outline is as follows:

Introduction
1. During my first week of graduate school, I had an immediate dislike for one of my classmates. Why?
2. At the same time, while working part-time on the local newspaper, I developed a subsurface anger toward my newly promoted supervisor, a young man who had been a friendly colleague the year before. Why?
3. Who are you angry with these days, and why?
    a. In your family, with whom do you find yourself bickering and quarreling, and why?
    b. When you gather with your relatives, with whom are you upset? Why?
    c. At school, who are the students or teachers that make you mad? Why?
    d. At the company you work for, in the office you go to, whom do you dislike and try to have the least contact with. Why?
    e. In the group you belong to—whether PTA, Junior League, Booster Club, task force, planning committee, sports club, Sunday school class, or church—with whom are you angry or irritated? Why?
4. What causes us to be angry, to fight, to quarrel, to hope someone gets taken down a peg or two?
5. Our quick answer is, "I'm angry because they did such and such." We dislike them because of some action on their

part. (Return to the examples above and describe the perceived offensive actions.)

6. But Scripture says there are more penetrating reasons why we are angry with some people, and these reason are not in them, but in us.

7. What are the reasons for our fights and quarrels, and what can we do about it? What are the causes, and what is the cure (inductive raising of the subject/question, and inductive previews of the coming main points)?

8. These are the questions James asks and answers in the fourth chapter of his letter. Please turn there.

I. There are two reasons why we fight and quarrel (Inductive).
   A. The first reason we fight and quarrel is because our desires are being denied (James 4:1–2a) (deductive).
      1. We have a strong self-centered desire for something, and the other person is denying or preventing us from having it, or perhaps getting it instead of us.
         a. (Explain the phrases of James 4:1–2a.)
         b. (Illustrate this denial in the examples given above.)
      2. Our response is to quarrel, fight, and "kill"—to wish them ill, and perhaps even attempt to bring them down by word or action.
   B. The second reason we fight and quarrel is because we no longer trust God for our legitimate desires, but have instead embraced the world's illicit values and aggressive behaviors (deductive).
      1. (Read and explain James 4:2b–5.)
      2. (Describe how these factors are operating in the examples used earlier.)
II. The cure to a fighting, quarreling spirit is a humble trust that God will grace our life (deductive statement of the big idea).
   A. (Explain the meaning of James 4:6 in light of Proverbs 3:33–35.)
   B. (Apply this answer to the examples mentioned earlier.)

The introduction sets up an overall inductive structure by focusing on the questions to be answered (Introduction 7). Since there is no particular advantage to deductively stating the big idea at the start, this inductive approach will better sustain the listener's attention. The answers to the questions, and the eventual big idea, will emerge as the message progresses.

The same questions (Introduction 7) also serve to inductively preview the main movements of the message, thus organizing the material to come.

The first movement (I.) is approached inductively, since the subpoints (IA. and IB.) are a list. But note that the submovement (IA.) is developed deductively, since its subpoints (IA1. and IA2.) are a logical progression, a chain of reasoning.

The message climaxes with a deductive statement of the big idea (II.), thus completing the overall inductive structure.

Conclusion

Through all these various levels in the message, the use of deduction and induction enables the speaker to "stick to the plot"—faithful to the biblical author, clear and relevant to the contemporary listener.

For Further Reflection

Getting the Idea

1. What is this chapter talking about?
2. What is this chapter saying about what it's talking about?

Building on the Idea

1. How important is the development of a clear flow to a message? Why?

2. What are the characteristics and advantages of a deductively shaped sermon?
3. What are the characteristics and advantages of an inductively shaped sermon?

Recommended Reading

Buttrick, David. *Homiletic*. Philadelphia: Fortress, 1987.
Cox, James. *Preaching*. San Francisco: Harper & Row, 1985.
Craddock, Fred B. *Overhearing the Gospel*. Nashville: Abingdon, 1978.
Lewis, Ralph. *Inductive Preaching*. Westchester, Ill.: Crossway, 1983.
Lowry, Eugene. *The Homiletical Plot*. Atlanta: John Knox, 1980.

9

Preaching for a Change

Joseph M. Stowell III

Crafting sermons to effect change requires that we stand before our people vulnerable and exposed. Vulnerable because we wield a tool that the Spirit uses as a surgical instrument in resistant hearts. Exposed because preaching for a change requires us to reveal slices of our own imperfect lives as fellow strugglers in the process of growth.

Preaching to convey information is predictable and unthreatening. Preaching to effect transformation is hard work and risky business. Yet that is the whole point of preaching. An effective sermon is measured not by its polished technique but by the ability of the preacher to connect the Word to the reality of the listener's life. Preachers and sermons can be funny, entertaining, enthralling, intriguing, intellectually stimulating, controversial, full of impressive theological and doctrinal footpaths, and authoritative. But if ultimately the outcome does not result in a changed life because of an encounter with truth, then it has not been what God intended preaching to be.

Real preaching forges a partnership with the piercing two-edgedness of the Word. It lifts the Word like a revealing mirror, lets it flow like cleansing water, and allows it to enter hearts like a seed ready to germinate to fruits of righteousness.

While few of us will ever be great preachers, all of us can be effective. Effectiveness focuses on the intended results of preaching. The end game of God's Word is not just to make us smart or theologically astute but rather to effect change. It is about leading listeners to change their minds and hearts. To repent of sin. To relate to God and others more constructively. To grow in our capacity to reflect the reality of Christ in our lives. To think more clearly about him and who he is. To think more clearly about who we really are.

This kind of effectiveness begins by bringing the appropriate perspective to the task. There are two competing perspectives of preaching: viewing preaching as a profession or as a purpose-driven expression of our gifts. The professional asks, "How well did I preach?" The purpose-oriented proclaimer asks, "How are my listeners doing?" and, "How well is Christ able to effect his or her transformational power through me?" The professional focuses on performance. The effective preacher focuses on power.

I recently visited a church whose pastor is known as a leading communicator. I deeply admire his gifts. It was a midweek service in which people were sharing testimonies about the previous Sunday's services. A man stood up and exclaimed, "Bill, ten minutes into the sermon you disappeared, and I began to hear the voice of God in my life."

I want to preach like that.

If they never know our names or remember who we are, effective preachers are fulfilled when lives are impacted by an encounter with the living God through his Word. Pastor Jay Jentink wrote to me that his greatest joy is "seeing God change people! There is something so incredible about watching a person who moves from a disinterest in God to intense commitment. The joy comes from knowing it is a privilege to have a place in God's plan for that person."

The purpose of the proclaimer is to connect with the listener as a conduit, not a celebrity. It is to impress people with the greatness of his God, not the greatness of his gift.

To accomplish this, there are four dynamics that an effective preacher must cultivate. Surprisingly, the first dynamic has nothing to do with preaching. It relates to the kind of sermons we preach with our lives. Second, connecting demands that we align our messages with the transformational intentions of the Word. Third, effectiveness requires that we carefully focus our applications into the contexts of real-life experiences And, fourth, effectiveness requires that we wrap the finished product in the clarity of applicational techniques.

The Preacher

As in any trade, the sharpness and adeptness of the craftsperson is critically important. In 1 Timothy 4:12–13 Paul instructs Timothy that personhood precedes proclamation. As Paul notes, lives that are exemplary in speech, conduct, love, faith, and purity will capture the attention of listeners and open the door of their desire to change. There is no doubt that our lives are the most important sermon that we preach. People are observers first and listeners second. Fewer things damage transformational proclamation more quickly than a proclaimer whose life contradicts what he preaches. Yet, when people watch us and want to grow as we are, the sermon serves to tell them how.

It will come as a relief to note that we are not talking about perfection. What is required, however, is a life that is authentic in its struggle and clearly marked by progress. Paul concludes: "Take pains with these things . . . so that your progress may be evident to all. Pay close attention to yourself and to your teaching and persevere in these things" (1 Tim. 4:15–16).

The Text

The second critical element in transformational proclamation is the crafting of a sermon that aligns itself with the life-changing power of the text. Paul instructs Timothy to "give attention to the public reading of scripture, to exhortation and teaching" (1 Tim. 4:13). The text must permeate our preparation and presentation. Sermons that deal only lightly or obscurely with the text cannot achieve the purpose of long-term, life-changing results. Our power is not in the clever creations of the communicator but in the intrinsic power of the truth of the Word of God.

The life-changing power of the Word ignites when both the purposes and the process of the text are embraced in the sermon. First, let's look at the purposes with a view to cooperating with them in our preaching.

Purposes

Exhortation and Teaching. As Paul notes "exhortation and teaching" are two critically important purposes in the presentation of the Word. Exhortation involves applying Scripture to a person's real-life situation with the goal of moving that individual toward maturity in Christ. Teaching, on the other hand, involves the clear communication of scriptural fact and biblical data in its appropriate theological context. An effective sermon cannot consist of exhortation without teaching nor can it be teaching without exhortation.

We need to work hard to make sure our listeners are engaged in these two strategic purposes. Teaching helps listeners come to grips with what the text is saying; exhortation empowers them to understand what the text is saying to them in a way that can change their lives. While it is true that the two dynamics merge at times, by and large teaching relates to information and exhortation to transformation.

The successful integration of both teaching and exhortation into our preaching requires that we understand that sermon preparation is both a science and an art. The science side of preaching deals with the exegesis of the text. It mines accurate information from the text based on historical, grammatical, contextual, and cultural research and isolates the central idea in the text.

The art side of preparation relates to transitioning this information into applicational packages that enable the listener to infuse the intent of the text into the context of his or her life. The science and the art of preparation are unalienable partners. Applications clearly grounded in the text ring truest in the hearts of believers.

Unfortunately, most of us feel that our sermon preparation is largely complete when the scientific enterprise of exegesis is done. Actually, we have only begun.

Preparing a sermon is like preparing a meal. We get the recipe out, shop for the necessary ingredients, and bring home bags full of all the right stuff. At that point, having set the ingredients on the counter, we are not at the end of the process. We don't ask our guests to grab a can of tomatoes and a little cream and make soup for themselves. Nevertheless, that's what happens in many of our sermons when we stop at the end of our exegesis and then lay out the message in its informational form, making little or no effort to connect the truth to life.

The challenge to every sermon preparer is the challenge of making an accurate transition from the exegesis stage to the applicational stage, from the scientific work to the artistry of the sermon. The transition begins by restating the central idea and the exegetical outline in terms of the real-life situations of the listener.

For instance, an exegetical point gleaned from Philippians 1:12ff. might be, "Paul relates his personal perspective in the midst of great difficulty." While this is good information, it doesn't help the listener apply the message to contemporary life settings. Instead, we need to present this information in an applicational format. Something like, "When our perspective is right, we can sense delight in the midst of difficulty," draws the listener in. Note that applicational points have personal pronouns that relate to the listener rather than the author ("we" instead of "Paul"; "our" instead of "his"), focusing the text on the experience of the listener rather than the experience of the author.

Four Functional Purposes. As we work toward integrating the purposes of exhortation and teaching into our sermons it is critical that we do so in intentional cooperation with the transformational functions of scripture. In 2 Timothy 3:16, 17, Paul lists four additional purposes that make God's Word effective in empowering individuals to change.

The first dynamic is teaching. Teaching in this context transitions listeners from their ignorance in old, false views that governed their previous life in the dark system of Satan to an educated understanding of kingdom truth about God, themselves, and the world in which they live.

The second objective is reproof. This is the confrontational work of God's Word, which reveals the shortfalls in our lives. The Word proclaimed should connect with hidden faults and expose the shameful secrets in inner lives. God's Word accomplishes this without us having to point our biblical bazooka at suspect parishioners. We need to communicate the principles with clear, authoritative application—real-life examples of biblical truth in action or imperatives that grow out of the principles. His Word takes care of the rest.

The third transformational dynamic is correction. This is the quiet, careful nudging of the Word of God to keep us on track. Whereas reproof deals confrontationally with willful sin in our lives, correction is a more subtle influence on our spiritual walk. It checks our proneness to wander.

The fourth functional purpose of the Word of God is its ability to train us in righteousness. As a parent rears a child in what is right, so Scripture rears us through a maturing process toward living our lives according to the righteous standards of God

Since these are the divine intentions of the text, transformational proclaimers need to keep these purposes at the forefront as they prepare to communicate. Throughout the preparation of the sermon, an applicational preacher asks himself, "What are the specific teaching elements in this text? What is there in this text that would serve as a reproof? How would this correct a wandering life? What are the righteous standards that are raised on the landscape of this text? How can I enable and empower people to respond in a constructive way to these elements of change?"

When we begin to answer these questions for ourselves, we have begun to answer them for the listener.

Process

As proclaimers who focus our proclamations on the transformational purposes of Scripture, we need to be careful that we do not emphasize the product of a transformed life without guiding people through the biblical process that enables them to arrive at that destination. Hence Paul told Timothy to be committed to patient instruction (2 Tim. 4:2). Instruction is the art of taking the listener through the process that leads to change.

Clearly Paul was committed to instructing the readers of his epistles in the processes that led to the product of a sanctified life. Romans 6–8 is laden with biblical processes for the attainment of sanctification. This pattern is reflected consistently in Paul's letters. For instance, in Philippians 1:9–11, instead of demanding that his readers make excellent choices in their lives and live lives that were fruitful and glorifying to God, Paul instructed them first in the process. It was his prayer for them that they would have a growing love in the context of knowledge that was expressed in discernment. If they lived out those three processes well, they would automatically choose that which was excellent, reflect the fruits of righteousness, and bring glory and praise to Christ in their lives.

I remember talking with a retired gentleman who is now a consultant in quality control. Since I was a pastor at the time and considered pastoral ministry to be a matter of quality control I asked him about the basic principles that guided his consulting. He said, "In quality control, we're more concerned with the process than we are with the product. If the process is right the product is guaranteed." How profound!

Product-oriented exhortations will cause listeners no end of frustration. Crafting process-friendly instructions will enable and empower people to grow. Process-oriented proclaimers ask the question as they study the text, "What does this text say about how I can accomplish the spiritual goal in this text?" Sometimes the answer lies in the broader context of the paragraph we are preaching. At times it may be found in the broader context of the book. Sometimes it is expounded in parallel passages in Scripture that call for the same outcome but give greater detail about how to arrive at the desired end.

Aligning our sermons with the transformational dynamics of the purposes and process of the text will inevitably result in changed lives. As Paul told Timothy, the divinely intended outcome of the Word proclaimed is lives that are changed to produce good works (2 Tim. 3:17).

If we claim to be effective preachers then we have to demonstrate that in the lives of our listeners.

The Context

Not only does transformation depend on the quality of the proclaimer's life and a clear alignment with the intentions of Scripture, but it also gains power from the preacher's understanding of the context into which he preaches. The key issue here is how well sermons connect with the world in which parishioners live.

When *Forbes* magazine celebrated its seventy-fifth anniversary it did so with a special issue that focused on the theme, "Why Do We Feel So Bad When We Have It So Good?" *Forbes* invited nine authors, philosophers, psychologists, and poets to write a response to that probing question. Peggy Noonan, former CBS correspondent with Dan Rather and speechwriter for Presidents Reagan and Bush, was asked to be one of the contributors. In her article, "You'd Cry Too," she made a stunning observation regarding our culture that goes to the heart of the dilemma we face in a society that has shifted far from its moorings. She wrote, "I think we have lost the old knowledge that happiness is overrated, that, in a way, life is overrated. We have lost, somehow, a sense of mystery, about us, our purpose, our meaning, our role." She went on to say:

Our ancestors believed in two worlds, and understood this to be the solitary, poor, nasty, brutish, and short one. We are the first generation of man that actually expected to find happiness here on earth, and our search for it has caused much unhappiness. The reason: if you do not believe in another, higher world, if you believe only in the flat material world around you and if you believe that this is your only chance at happiness, if that is what you believe, then you are not disappointed when the world does not give you a good measure of its riches. You are despairing.

Peggy Noonan is a compelling model for transformational proclaimers. She has taken the time to understand the context of the culture into which she writes, and then with penetrating precision brings the truth to bear on the culture's dilemma.

Effectiveness demands that we as preachers go beyond the text to the context of the culture and our congregation. This is the point in the process where the preacher moves the changeless Word of God into the face of the real issues of the listener.

Every listener has three distinct contexts: personal, local, and universal. All three compete to form the attitudes, perceptions, and actions of the congregation. They create grids through which all the pulpit information is passed. These contexts have distinct codes and languages, doors, windows, and barriers and create a variety of passageways into the parishioners' hearts. Haddon Robinson has noted that the effective preacher must not only exegete the text, but the audience as well.

Personal Contexts

The shepherd-feeder has to relate in proclamation to a variety of people. Single. Happily married. Sadly married. Single parents. Divorcees. Widows. Widowers. Those who carry the secret of being abused and abusing. Those who come from horrendous backgrounds. Others who have happy, positive legacies through past generations. Some are struggling with lust and involved in illicit affairs. Cheating at the office. Disappointed with life and carrying deep-seated questions about God. Some are successful, complacent, and self-sufficient. Some are proud; others are going through humbling experiences. It would be helpful to observe people carefully and to keep a list of the various personal contexts that are represented in a congregation.

As we seek to connect applicationally, sensitivity to these contexts becomes strategically important. This is especially true when sermons deal with volatile issues like abortion, divorce, fathering, mothering, success, wealth, failure, and the like. For instance, when we preach against abortion, there will probably be some in the congregation who have had abortions. If we do not carefully craft the application in terms of their personal context we will unnecessarily compound their guilt and despair. What they really need to hear from us is that God values their life and will forgive, forget, and grant a second chance.

When we do a family series, those from broken homes will suffer through the whole sermon if we don't put in a disclaimer that wraps them in hope and understanding. Singles will feel marginalized. Sermons on parenting often create special grief for parents who already feel that they have failed or lost their children. Some note of biblical encouragement and perspective must be shared with them in the course of the application.

Illustrations, with all their capacity to open windows in our minds, sometimes offend personal contexts if they are not handled carefully. I have an illustration that I use about taking our children out for Halloween. Recognizing that some of my listeners would be horrified to think that our children went trick-or-treating, I used to throw in a disclaimer in the course of the illustration. Something like, "Now, I know how many of us feel about Halloween, so don't send me any letters." And then I would do a little aside about those who wreck our holidays by doing historical research on them. It always engendered understanding laughter and permitted me to go on with the illustration.

Recently, I got a three-page handwritten letter from a woman who started out by saying, "I know you said you didn't want any letters, and I know you don't like those who research the meanings of holidays, but I felt compelled to write to you anyway." She went on to tell of her childhood, growing up in a home where Satan was worshiped and how year after year on Halloween her family participated in satanic rituals where child sacrifice took place. She said, "For me, Halloween is not a joke, but a horrible memory that I struggle with to this day." You can count on the fact that I'll craft the articulation of that illustration differently the next time I use it.

Haddon Robinson says that as he is working on the application side of his sermon he mentally invites representatives of various contexts in his church to sit across the desk and interact with the text. He envisions a divorcée, a teenager, an older charter member, a successful businessperson, a recently unemployed individual, or any number of other persons, and listens to what they would ask and to how they would view the text. A tactic like Robinson's forces the transformational proclaimer into personal contexts, sharpens his sensitivities, and enables him to fine-tune his illustrations and applications accordingly. A context-sensitive preacher sees all of his applicational ammunition through the real-life settings that his listeners deal with on a day-to-day basis.

Local Context

Local contexts are broader than personal contexts and relate specifically to the environmental implications of particular communities and regions of the country. These local contexts deal with race, class, gender, politics, local history, and general civic environments.

If you minister in Grand Rapids, Michigan, for instance, your local context will be far different from that of Los Angeles or San Diego. Ministry in Boston has a far different context than ministry in Dallas. More liberal constituencies demand a perspective in applicational preaching that is different from that required in conservative contexts. The emphasis of transformational proclamation in a more liberal context would lean more toward righteousness and sensitivity to sin, whereas ministry in a conservative context would need to lean more toward applications dealing with compassion, justice, and freedom.

Contexts in which there is racial diversity will require specific applications that call for greater sensitivity toward others, cry out against the barriers of racial prejudice, and call people's attention to the unifying factor of our mutual allegiance to the cross and the person of Christ. Rural towns and urban settings call for different applications in sermons. Blue-collar areas are far different than professional areas. The teens bring their own local culture, as do the elderly, baby boomers, and busters. A good shepherd stays up to speed on the environment within which he proclaims.

I recall in my second pastorate referring on occasion to the *Wall Street Journal.* To my surprise, some in our congregation, including a staff member, expressed consternation that I would refer to the *Journal* in my sermons. While we had a scattering of professionals in the congregation, many were blue-collar workers and farmers. To them the references were out of their context. In fact they made me appear "uppity" and separated me from my people. Quoting from the *Journal* violated the local context.

Few of us would ever consider supporting a missionary who went to a field and did not minister within the context of the local language and cultural patterns. Similarly, we dare not ignore the importance of learning the life languages of our people and becoming students of the ever-changing environment of our culture, which has dramatically affected the mind-set, life patterns, and response mechanisms of those who hear.

Universal Context

Regardless of the diversities that are represented in personal and local contexts some contextual dynamics are universally experienced. Everyone wrestles with greed, hate, guilt, anger, prejudice, impatience, lust, procrastination, self-indulgence, and a propensity to be obsessed with enhancing and maintaining personal significance—or fighting the loss of it.

Effective sermons find these issues in the text and focus the application of the sermon on the biblical alternatives of kingdom qualities that are universally applicable, such as generosity, forgiveness, love, servanthood, and the like.

The effective proclaimer must also realize that in North America, at least, we live in the context of a story-oriented culture. In a context where illiteracy is on the increase, intellectual depth is on the decrease, and experience is the standard, people perceive stories as important vehicles of truth. Television, movies, and music are story-related. The evening news is a compilation of stories. Newspapers are stories in print. Great movies are extended stories. Even athletic contests are sprinkled with interviews with leading athletes that create stories behind the game. All of this presses us to learn to be effective storytellers in both the crafting and the delivery of our sermons. It calls us as well to capitalize on the story lines in Scripture. Storytelling is one of the proclaimer's most important connecting commodities.

Some of the clearest moments in Christ's communication were times when he told dramatic stories to illuminate a point. In Luke 15, instead of preaching a long, cognitive discourse on the importance of having compassion on the lost, he told three stories that proved his point. These stories stand today as outstanding moments in Christ's ministry and remain stories with which we are all familiar. And while a proclaimer must never let sermon time become story time, stories powerfully serve to illuminate, clarify, and drive the biblical point home.

Perhaps the most critical element of today's universal context has to do with values. Values shape us, mold us, drive us, and define us. The dramatic shift in values in America challenges the effective proclaimer to stay up to speed lest his communication seem irrelevant—not because of his biblical material but because of the pervasive influence that these changing values have on our listeners. If we are not helpful here we will put people in jeopardy of being sucked into the vortex of the new set of rules by which the general culture lives.

The applicational preacher looks at the text for references to biblical values that counteract the prevalent cultural values. He asks, "What are the values of our societal system that have become so influential in the lives of my flock?" And, "What are the countervalues of Scripture?"

For instance, transformational preaching must be ready to address the tension between . . .

. . . Temporalism and living in the light of eternity . . .

Peggy Noonan was right. We are the first generation to forget that there are two worlds, to believe only in the flat, material world around us, which, as she noted, has brought us such despair.

How many of our parishioners measure their life, success, and possessions in terms of a temporal perspective rather than an eternal perspective? As proclaimers we need to remediate this fallen part of our cultural value system by transitioning the hearts and minds of our people to eternity by weaving into our messages applications that force the perspectives of our hearers beyond the temporary to that which is eternal.

. . . Materialism as opposed to a spiritually prioritized life . . .

Having eliminated the preeminent value of eternal pursuits in our culture, we have dumbed ourselves into the assumption that fulfillment and satisfaction in life can be found in what we can gain, keep, and accumulate in terms of the material order. We need to be careful that we don't impose false guilt on those who, for reason of honest, astute business practices and the sovereign bestowal of God, have gained much in this world. The real point of materialism is not how much we have, but what has us. It's not what we hold, but how tightly we hold it. Not what we have, but how we got it. The test of materialism is whether our goods have made us proud or grateful, self-sufficient or God-sufficient.

Proclamation in this secular age must continue to point people to the values of godliness over gain, of personal piety over property, and of people over the stockpiles of things.

. . . Tolerance in counterdistinction to a gracious yet tenacious embrace of truth . . .

There is no doubt that the most celebrated value of our neo-pagan society is tolerance. Given the conclusion of relativism that there are no absolutes and the prevalent notion of post-modernism that there is no truth we are left to stand without judgment on anything. Nothing is right and nothing is wrong. To speak absolutes and to claim to know a true God who has communicated truth is a violation of the culture's allegiance to tolerance.

Unfortunately, many Christians have been influenced by this predominant value and have little stomach for specific applications of truth or for scrutinizing false belief systems by the authority of the Word. Christians are prone today to segment their beliefs by saying, "It's wrong for me, but I can't say that for everyone."

. . . Sensualism as opposed to self control . . .

Our society places high value on the stimulation of our senses, whether it be through thrill-a-minute horror and violence in the media, or by sexual satisfaction in any context and to any extent.

Standing in bold contrast is the biblical encouragement toward self-control, where we are to stimulate our senses with the presence of the indwelling Spirit and turn our impulses and passions toward loving what God loves and finding our fulfillment in doing His will.

. . . Hedonism as contrasted to finding pleasure in pleasing God . . .

Hedonism fans the flame of sensualism since it dedicates itself to the pursuit of pleasure regardless of the cost. It minimizes the consequences, seeks to erase the guilt, and invites people to enjoy. However, God calls his people to find their pleasure in bringing pleasure to him. In fact, that's how we're built. Just as a child finds his greatest pleasure in pleasing his parents, so we are to focus our attention not on pleasing ourselves, but on pleasing God and others on his behalf. This is the true source of pleasure.

. . . Self-centeredness rather than servanthood . . .

Narcissus is a mythological character who one day, walking by a still pool of water, looked in, saw his face, and immediately fell in love with himself. He became preoccupied with himself and found himself often wanting to go to the pond to see himself again. Our culture fans the flames of this preoccupation with self by preaching the importance of self-advancement, self-enhancement, and self-fulfillment. It's the old "Look Out for #1" syndrome, which has led our culture to clamor for personal rights, privileges, and recognition.

Scripture lifts the biblical value of servanthood as the antidote to the values of a narcissistic world. The best thing, according to Jesus Christ, is to give the treasure of self totally to God, and then, in turn, as an expression of our love to God, give it to others (Matt. 22:34–40). True fulfillment and satisfaction come not by heaping all of life upon self, but rather by giving self away. By serving, not by being served.

Other values like autonomy in the place of submission and community; self-consumption in the place of love for others; greed instead of generosity; violence instead of protection and stewardship; consumerism rather than making a contribution create a threatening context for the believer to live in. Those of us who are dedicated to transforming lives through the proclamation of the Word of God need to keep these kind of value conflicts in mind as we study the text. Our task is to enable people to know, understand, and embrace the biblical values that replace these secular rules. Ongoing exposure to the countervalues of Scripture Sunday after Sunday should press listeners out of their cultural context. Maturing believers need to be taught to identify and reject false values and to live by authentically biblical values.

It would be well to prepare each text with these questions in mind:

1. What biblical value is taught in this text?
2. What is the countervalue our culture promotes?
3. How will this message:
   a. define, articulate, and illustrate this biblical value?
   b. address the countervalue?
   c. encourage and enable Christians to transition from one to the other?

Clarity

All of our efforts to come to grips with personhood, the text, and the context demand that we present our material to the listener with life-related clarity. It's surprising to discover that when we think our presentation is clear, in reality it may not be clear at all. The most discouraging compliment I ever hear is, "Thank you for that sermon. It was really deep." That usually means the person couldn't understand it

Here are some key ingredients that bring clarity to a transformational message. First the structural elements (i.e., introduction, main points, transitions, conclusion) must be oriented to application rather than information. This takes place when all the key elements of the sermon address the listener and move with the listener toward the transformational point of the message.

Applicational Points

No doubt the most important aspect of clarity is the formation of a concise, memorable, applicational statement of the central idea. While the exegetical statement of the central idea may be "Christ elevates servanthood as an imperative," an applicational version might be "The authentic Christian descends into greatness." The same type of spin needs to be reflected in our main points, transitions, introductions, and conclusions.

Ask the question, "How can this point focus on the listener?" Craft the statement in a precise and penetrating way. Don't be cute. The concept needs to be carried in a vehicle that honors its importance. Work hard at this. It's the artistry that drives the message all the way home.

Applicational Illustrations

As we have already seen, because we live in a story-oriented culture, the effective preacher must hone his skills as a storyteller. This brings us to the role of illustrations. The best illustrations are ones to which people can relate. Illustrations drawn from weekly newspapers, daily family life, TV, movies (when appropriate), and personal experiences are effective if they are presented carefully and in the right context. Something from that Sunday's morning paper is especially hot.

If the illustrations are taken from family or personal experience, particularly if they reflect positively on our lives, we need to be careful that they don't set us up as unrealistic examples of spiritual success. Sometimes a disclaimer like "I wish I were always this successful in my walk with Christ" might be appropriate in front of a story that talks about a personal spiritual victory. Stories that share our faults should not be so specific that they erode the congregation's confidence in us. We don't need to tell all of our struggles in vivid detail. At the same time, it is important that the congregation knows that we struggle with the same kinds of things they struggle with.

The most important thing to remember about illustrations is that they must clearly focus on the point we are making It's great to have a smashing story, but if it doesn't fit it will only serve to distract attention from the point we are trying to drive home. And, we must resist using the strongest story of the message to illustrate a minor point. Illustrations need to carry equal weight with the weight of the moment in the message. If you want the listener to go home remembering something less than the central idea then misplace a heavyweight illustration.

The best illustrations never need to be explained. If we have to say at the end of the illustration, *What this means is. . .* , it probably has not been a good illustration.

Partnering with illustrations is the use of word pictures and metaphors that are consistent with the context of the listener's experience.

Applicational Introductions

The introduction must be crafted to set the stage for the transformational point that will be made in the development of the central idea of the text. A sermon that starts applicationally will set the stage of the hearer's heart to taking a step of maturity during the message. Introductions should be crisp, interesting, and provocative and provide an effective orientation to what is to come. You know the introduction is effective when the listener wants to go with you into the message.

Applicational Conclusions

A good conclusion rearticulates the central idea of the text applicationally and packages the main points in a brief and memorable way. A good applicational conclusion moves the listeners toward a resolve for change in their lives and suggests ways in which they can apply the text in the coming hours or days.

A good conclusion may include such questions as, "Since we have learned that purity is the pilgrim's priority, what difference will this make in your thought life this week?" It's important at that point to give your listeners a moment to interact with the question as they form their own plans of action. We can encourage a transformational response by saying something like, "Before you go to work tomorrow morning, write down one way in which a commitment to purity will change your attitude toward those you work with." A good applicational conclusion summarizes the truth of the text and launches applicational plans by which the listener can effectively transform his or her life into greater conformity with the will and glory of God.

Applicational Programming

A preacher committed to change in listeners' lives searches for programmatic ways to expand the influence of the text. Bulletin inserts can focus on take-home applications. If the configuration of your Sunday worship service permits, a special elective after the sermon for people interested in reviewing the principles and discussing personal applications can provide interesting and productive interaction.

If you have a Sunday evening service, or a small-group emphasis it can be effective to use these times to deal with specific applications in greater depth or to consider other portions of Scripture that speak to the theme. A panel of laypersons could be effective in discussing ways the sermon could be implemented in their own lives, and in turn help others glean new insights and applications

If you are involved in a series of sermons around particular themes, testimonies might be used as a part of the worship service to focus on victories and/or challenges that people in the church are experiencing as a result of seeking to apply the themes to their lives.

A proclaimer cannot do enough to enable his messages to move through the mind and heart of the listener all the way to a changed life.

Concluding Thoughts

The most powerful sermons are forged out of the heart of a preacher who has sought to live out the principle of the text in the week or weeks prior to its presentation. Sermons forged in life smack of the reality of life and will find easy transition into the life of the listener. Sermons formed only in the mind of the preacher will probably affect little more than the mind of the listener.

While it is true that transformation is the work of the text under the guidance of the Holy Spirit and that it is he who will ultimately do the work of convicting, comforting, healing, helping, encouraging, motivating, and transforming; it is also true that our messages are the conduit. We craft the instrument. He is the enablement. Our challenge is to do our best to create a useful tool in the Master's hand. When we are successful we enjoy the satisfaction of preaching for a change.

For Further Reflection

Getting the Idea

1. What is this chapter talking about?
2. What is this chapter saying about what it's talking about?

Building on the Idea

1. What changes are needed in your preaching to make it more transformational?
2. What role does prayer play in transformational preaching?
3. List some "personal contexts" to whom you preach.

Recommended Reading

Briscoe, D. Stuart. *Fresh Air in the Pulpit*. Grand Rapids: Baker; Leicester: Inter-Varsity Press, 1994.

Larsen, David L. *Caring for the Flock*. Wheaton: Crossways, 1991.

Larsen, David L. *The Evangelism Mandate: Recovering the Centrality of Gospel Preaching*. Wheaton: Crossways, 1992.

Stowell, Joseph M. *Shepherding the Church*. Chicago: Moody, 1997.

Willhite, Keith. "Stop Preaching in the Dark." *Preaching* (May–June), pp. 15–16.

Visualizing the Big Idea

Stories That Support Rather Than Steal

John W. Reed

My association with Haddon Robinson began in 1970, when I joined the faculty at Dallas Theological Seminary. After eight satisfying years in the pastorate and nine years of teaching homiletics and communication at Cedarville College, I was ready for a seminary position. My graduate work in communication at two universities had taught me that the process of effective sermon construction was knowing the right questions to ask. Every system of homiletical theory that I had uncovered left me without those questions. Cedarville College graduates who had studied under Haddon Robinson at Dallas Seminary assured me that he had found them.

During that first year in the classroom at Dallas Seminary I discovered that Haddon Robinson had indeed found these questions and was apt to teach them. My task was to evaluate the sermons preached by students who had been through Robinson's first course. They graciously explained to me how his system worked. They understood his approach and taught me. If my threat level had been very high, I wouldn't have survived the first semester. It was several months before I could produce a sermon outline that revealed that I understood the process. I'm glad for God's and Haddon Robinson's grace during my learning period. Nearly three decades have passed and I have yet to find a more effective homiletical approach.

Early in my experience with Haddon Robinson I discovered how greatly he valued illustrations. He regularly collected and filed illustrations. All homiletics students were required to practice this fine art. "Collect and file at least five illustrations every week," was Haddon Robinson's sage advice. Over the years I have talked with several of these students who have done so. Their collections now contain thousands of well-selected stories and quotations.

Let me propose a simple test for a powerful sermon. Try *not* listening to the preacher. I once had a pastor I could not avoid listening to. Sometimes I would come into the worship service distracted and wanting to think about something besides his sermon. He grabbed my attention immediately and would not let me go. If I tried to turn my mind in a different direction, he kept jerking my attention back. When I analyzed the reason for this gripping experience, I discovered that the key was his excellent choice and use of illustrations—illustrations that supported his idea.

Illustration Defined

At this point it is important to define what I mean by the term "illustration." *The American Heritage Dictionary* gives three levels of definition for the word. All three are pertinent to our discussion, although the third would appear at first to be unrelated. These are the three: 1. Illustration is the act of clarifying or explaining. 2. Illustrations are the material used to clarify or explain. 3. Illustrations can be visual matter used to clarify or decorate a text. (Think of the text as meaning a sermon.)

First, illustration is the act of clarifying or explaining. That concept is closely related to the word "exposition" and is certainly appropriate to expository preaching. In other words, illustration is a natural part of biblical exposition. However, as part of the discussion concerning illustrating sermons, we should add one more factor to this first phase of the definition. Illustration can also be an effective means of application. The primary definition as amended would read as follows: Illustration is the act of clarifying, explaining, or applying.

Second, the word "illustration" can describe any materials used to clarify or explain. Again I would add application. In fact a choice illustration could achieve all three of these objectives at one time. The right story or case history could effectively clarify, explain, and apply. Here is an example of an illustration that could carry this threefold responsibility:

> As a young farm boy in north central Ohio, I remember going with my father to watch harness racing at the county fair. Dad taught me the evils of gambling but also the joy of seeing well-bred horses run. These were trotting horses. Each horse pulled a sulky in which the driver was seated. As the horses ran, their heads seemed to float around the track. On the far side of the oval they presented a beautiful picture of unity and purpose. I knew they were competing for the prize, but it was an unforgettable image of a group heading for the same goal.
>
> Sometimes a horse would break stride. When that happened, the horse's head reared up. The unity was clearly broken and the scene was marred. When one horse broke stride, those near would often follow the lead. The scene of tranquil unity changed to chaos. Often there would be a wreck with injury to the horses and drivers. In a similar way the unity of the church is marred when individual members break stride with God and fellow members. Their rebellion usually causes others to follow. Chaos can result.
>
> It is comforting to know that a horse that has broken stride, if it submits to the direction of the driver, can regain stride. It is even possible for the restored horse to win the race. That should be an encouragement to us all.

There are probably no perfect illustrations. This one might be used in a discussion of harmony or unity of purpose. It could be used to clarify, explain, or apply, or to do all three at once. It would be effective to use the first part of the illustration in the introduction and use the restoration portion later in the message. The renewal emphasis would fit nicely in the conclusion. Its use there would bring the sermon full circle and give a sense of completeness to the message. This kind of illustration might be called a major metaphor. Its presence is felt throughout the sermon and more than one reference may be made to it, helping to bring into focus the central idea.

The third part of the definition affirms that illustrations are visual matter used to clarify or decorate a text. Obviously the dictionary definition had in mind the use of pictures or other forms of graphic art intended to show aspects of the meaning discussed in the text of oral or written discourse. In a sermon the illustration that is needed often takes the form of a word picture or story. Part of the divine creation is the blessing of being able to see pictures in our heads. This has been called in popular language "using the mind's eye."

Pictures in the Mind

A Christian psychologist, Frank Wichern, once told me that he could tell whether a client was lying to him in a counseling session. When a person was lying the counselor couldn't see a picture of the event being related in his head. If the experience being related actually happened the picture of the event appeared on the visual screen in the mind of the psychologist.

This reality of creation was brought home to me several years ago when I was teaching a college course in oral interpretation of literature. I had been teaching the concept of esthetic distance. The idea of this is that when reading a selection of literature aloud, the reader should keep an emotional distance so as not to lose control. If a reader or speaker breaks down with emotion, the effect on the audience is lost.

Irene was a very gifted oral reader who was a member of the class. She had great natural ability and was one of the stars. She came to me and asked whether she should read a poem entitled

"Little Boy Blue" by Eugene Field. It was a short poem about a family that had lost a little boy through death. The parents refused to change anything in the boy's room because they couldn't cope with their loss. It was a very emotional piece.

Irene said, "I have had a similar experience in my life and I'm not sure that I can handle the emotional impact."

I told her that she alone could decide. I then explained that if she read the poem aloud many times in rehearsal the esthetic distance could make it possible for her to handle the emotion during performance. Irene prepared and read the selection in class. There were forty students enrolled in the class and most of them were present the day this event took place. As she read a phenomenon took place in our minds that is referred to as recall and transference. The members of the class saw the images on the screens of their minds and clothed the images with the trappings of their own experience. This made the experience much more intimate and powerful.

As Irene read the poem I saw the room in which my brother had grown up. It was a dynamic image and was generating a strong level of emotional impact. The poem was about three minutes long. About two-thirds of the way though Irene's reading, the scene in my mind suddenly went blank. I struggled to pull back the image and couldn't. Irene continued to read. Her vocal and physical response was unaltered but the screen of my mind stayed blank.

When she finished, I stood before the class and asked, "Did anything happen to you during the reading?"

The class responded in unison, "The picture disappeared. The screen went blank."

I said to Irene, "What happened?"

She replied, "You said that I might lose control while reading this emotional poem. That began to happen to me so I turned it off."

I asked Irene what she had turned off. She didn't know. What I now understand is that there exists in all of us the ability to use what is called eidetic imagery. This is an inner sensory projector that is in operation naturally when we are sincerely relating an illustration or story.[1] If we are lying about a personal incident, it appears that this projection process from the mind of the reader or speaker is not in operation. That helps us understand how the psychologist I mentioned earlier can tell when a client is lying to him.

It has been my observation that eidetic imagery fails to operate in other situations as well. If I do not have mastery of the material I am presenting, the image will be blurred in my own mind and therefore also in the mind of the audience members. As in the case cited of Irene there also appears to be the ability in some people to "turn off" or negate the effectiveness of eidetic imagery as a form of self-protection against loss of esthetic distance.

It can help us all immeasurably in our preaching if we think in terms of painting word pictures that will bring vibrant scenes to life in the minds of our listeners. The central issue seems to be that if I concentrate on the illustration I am relating, I should see it in my head. In the delivery of illustrations to an audience the most important element is concentration. But, then, concentration is a primary element in the mastery of any art. I helped my youngest grandson in his schoolwork by telling him to think about what he was thinking about when he was thinking about it. *That* is concentration.

In summary, illustrations are used in expository sermons to clarify, explain, or apply the idea. The most powerful form of illustration is the word picture that takes the idea being presented and makes it appear in the minds of audience members in vivid force. We should test all our illustrations by asking the simple question, "Does this put a picture in their heads? Is it the right picture, supporting the big idea?"

The Available Means of Persuasion

In order to validate the reality of the absolute importance of dynamic word pictures in expository preaching, I call to witness the impressive evidence developed over two thousand years of rhetorical history. In my graduate work I majored in classical rhetoric. I discovered that expository preaching has at its heart the expressed desire to persuade the audience to replace their attitudes, beliefs, and behaviors with those recommended in the sermon.

Communication theory recognizes three primary means of persuasion. These are ethical, emotional, and logical appeals. Ethical appeal is that which has its source in the person who is preaching the sermon at the time of preaching. Aristotle, in *The Rhetoric,* observed that people tend to believe speakers of known character and recognized achievements and who revealed love for the audience. Character is the foundation of persuasive power. Ethical appeal is the most powerful means of persuasion. Examples of moral failure in the lives of preachers verify that when character is gone, persuasive appeal is nullified.

The second most effective means of persuasion is emotional appeal. There are two primary aspects in developing this appeal. First, emotional appeal is developed by the preacher who reveals genuine conviction and enthusiasm or passion for the sermon being preached. The other primary means of developing emotional appeal is through the choice and use of illustrations. To develop powerful emotional appeal the preacher should recreate emotion-producing narrations of human experience. In other words, dynamic storytelling can be a powerful force in moving people to the desired response.

Many of you will reject this truth by saying that you want people to make logical, not emotional, decisions. My response to you is that most of us are so weak in this important discipline that we are not in danger of pushing anyone into an emotional decision. In fact, our storyless sermons are so boring people usually think about something else while we are preaching. Our real problem is that we don't understand emotional proof well enough to be effective communicators. As I reflect on the powerful expositors of Scripture I have heard over the past fifty years, most have been great storytellers. (I will have more to say about this shortly.)

The third means of persuasion is very important but is far weaker than ethical or emotional appeal. Logical appeal requires the preacher to find evidence in support of the assertions presented in the sermon and to reason effectively from this evidence. For the biblical expositor, the Bible is the primary means of evidence. This fact alone gives profound verification to the importance of biblical exposition. But it also condemns as essentially inadequate seminary training that does not emphasize character development and training in storytelling along with biblical studies.

Primary Elements of Illustrating Sermons

Since it is impossible for me to say everything about choosing and using illustrations, I will restrict myself to those elements that I consider most important. I have chosen to use examples from that great master of illustration, D. L. Moody. I feel that makes him an excellent mentor to all of us who preach in our generation.[2] Notice the anecdotal and personal interest nature of his illustrations.

I. To be effective in illustrating use concrete examples.

Be concrete! This could also be called the specific instance or the case study technique. This is the fundamental requirement of all good illustrations. Ronald Reagan understood this principle. In describing childlike faith Moody chose the following illustration:

"There is a man living in the city of New York who has a home on the Hudson River. His daughter and her family went to spend the winter with him: and in the course of the season a scarlet fever epidemic broke out. One little girl was put in quarantine, to be kept separate from the rest. Every morning the grandfather used to go and bid his grandchild, 'Good-by,' before going to his business.

"On one of these occasions the little girl took the man by the hand, and, leading him to a corner of the room, without saying a word she pointed to the floor where she had arranged some small crackers so they would spell out, 'Grandpa, I want a box of paints.'

"He said nothing. On his return home he hung up his overcoat and went to the room as usual; when his little grandchild, without looking to see if her wish had been complied with, took him into the same corner, where he saw spelled out in the same way, 'Grandpa, I thank you for the box of paints.' The grandfather would not have missed gratifying the child for anything. That was faith on the part of the grandchild."

II. To be effective in illustrating use human interest stories of real people resolving crises.

Tell about real people solving problems! Tell stories of people doing things right in the power of God. Don't be afraid of negative examples. Let the positive dominate. The following illustration reveals Moody at his very best:

"Dr. Willie Arnot, one of the greatest Scotch preachers, told me that his mother died when he was a little boy. There was a large family of Arnots. They all missed the tenderness and love of their mother. They got the impression that their father was very stern and rigid, and that he had a great many laws and rules. One rule was that the children should never climb trees.

"When the neighbor boys found out that the Arnot children could not climb trees, they explained that climbing trees was just about the best thing a boy could ever do. They told them about the wonderful things they could see from the tops of the trees. Well, tell a boy that he musn't climb a tree, and he will get up that tree some way. And so the Arnot children were all the time teasing their father to let them climb trees; but their father always said, 'No.'

"One day he was busy reading his newspaper, and the boys said: 'Father is reading his paper. Let's slip down into the lot and climb a tree.' Willie stood on the top of the stone fence to see that their father did not catch them. When his brother got up on the first branch, he said, 'What do you see?' 'Why! I don't see anything.' 'Then go higher; you haven't got high enough.' So up he went higher, and again Willie asked, 'Well, what do you see now?' 'I don't see anything.' 'You aren't high enough; go higher.'

And the little fellow went up as high as he could go, but he slipped, and down he came, and broke his leg. Willie said he tried to get him into the house, but he couldn't do it. He had to tell his father all about it. He said he was scared nearly out of his wits. He thought his father would be very angry. But he went in and confessed everything. His father surprised him. He just threw aside the paper, and started for the lot. When he got there, he picked the wounded brother up in his arms, and brought him to the house. Then he sent for the doctor and Willie said, "It seemed like my father was my mother." Willie had got a new view of his father. He found out the reason his father was so stern. The rules were for their protection and guidance."

III. To be effective in illustrating touch people emotionally.

Be personal! This is the heart of emotional appeal. Moody was a master of this. Here are some examples:

"A little child in Chicago, whose parents were unbelievers and had never taught her even the name of God, was dying. She opened her eyes, raised her hands, and said, 'Julia is coming, God.' Who taught her that there was a God who would receive little children? Her parents learned from her beautiful death to trust in Jesus."

Like Billy Graham, Moody placed great emphasis on God's love for all people. Here is one his most powerful experiences: "We were once erecting a tabernacle in Chicago, and a businessman said to me, 'I would like to put up a text on the wall of that building.' I supposed he was going to put up a motto in fine fresco. But I soon found the gas-fitter was working back of the pulpit. 'What are you doing?' I said. 'Putting in gas jets,' he replied. Our building was to be lighted by gas lights. And, to my amazement, I found he was putting up the motto 'GOD IS LOVE,' in gas jets so that it was impossible to light the church without lighting that text.

"One night a man was going by and he saw the gas-lighted text 'GOD IS LOVE,' and he said to himself, 'God is love, God is love.' By and by he came back, and he looked at it again. I saw him come in and take a seat by the door. Soon he put his hands up to his face, and once in a while I would see tears running down his cheeks, and I was foolish enough to think they were caused by my preaching.

After the service I went to him and said, 'What is the trouble?' 'I don't know.' 'What was there in the sermon that made you cry?' 'I didn't know you had been preaching.' 'Well, what was it that troubled you; was it anything in the songs?' 'I don't know anything about the songs.' 'Well,' I said, 'what is the matter?' 'That text up there,' he replied. 'My man,' I said, 'do you believe that God loves you.' 'I am not worth loving.' 'That's true,' I said, 'but he loves you all the more.' And I sat there a half-hour, and the truth of God's love shone into his soul and he became a new man.'"

IV. To illustrate effectively use comparison and contrast.

Compare and contrast! Moody was a master in using illustrations that hold interest by skillful use of contrast. Here is a story related to sheep and shepherds. "A lady in England was out riding and she saw a shepherd who had some dogs driving sheep. If the sheep stopped to drink out of the pools in the streets, he would have the dogs after them. She kept saying to herself, 'Oh, you cruel man!' But by-and-by the shepherd came to a beautiful park, opened the great iron gate, and let all the sheep in there where the grass was knee high, sweet, fresh grass, and a beautiful river running right through the park; and she said, 'He isn't a cruel shepherd after all. He didn't want them to eat and drink by the roadside where danger lurked. He was only trying to get them to a better place.'"

V. To illustrate effectively use dynamic imagery.

Create images! Moody said. "I once heard of two men who were under the influence of liquor. They came down at night to where their boat was tied. They wanted to return home, so they got in and began to row. They pulled away hard all night, wondering why they never got to the other side of the bay. When the gray dawn of morning broke, behold! they had never loosed the mooring line or raised the anchor! That's just the way with many who are striving to enter the kingdom of heaven. They cannot believe, because they are tied to this world. Cut the cord! Confess and forsake your sins! Cut the cord! Set yourselves free from the clogging weight of earthly things, and you will soon rise heavenward."

The Power of Positive Examples

There are many other issues that could be discussed about choosing and using illustrations. These I consider the core issues. You may feel that I have overstated the importance of concrete examples, human interest stories, and creating images in the minds of audience members. Try doing it and see what happens. Let your primary emphasis be on stories of people doing things right in the power of God.

Robert Schuller learned the power of positive thinking from Norman Vincent Peale. I am not advocating that our sermons be all case studies like those of Peale. However, it is important that we recognize it was this factor that made Peale so appealing. People understood what he was telling them to do. They had concrete images in their minds of how to do it. That is the point we shouldn't miss.

The first time I heard Bill Gothard speaking in what he then called Basic Youth Conflicts, I was struck by his persistent use of positive case studies. I vividly recall a series of films featuring James Dobson. Each of his lectures was filled with concrete case studies. It was impossible to not listen to him. You may say that these men are not preachers. That is true. But can't we preachers learn from them the importance of applying biblical preaching through case studies of people doing the things we advocate in the power of God's Spirit?

Nor do I wish to neglect the importance of the negative side. The Bible contains a good balance of positive examples and warning passages. In 1 Corinthians 10:1–13 the Apostle Paul lists an

extended series of Old Testament images that are negative examples. In verse 6 he reminds us that these images are warnings not
to do as they did. Contrast that passage with Hebrews 11, and
see the long series of positive images of people doing things right
in the power of faith. In like manner we should balance negative
and positive images. But in Scripture as in contemporary life, let's
emphasize the positive. Each negative in Scripture has as its
intention the practice of the positive alternative as seen in 1 Corinthians 10:13.

The Bible is primarily a book of case histories. While there are
many negative examples the driving force is for believers to obey
God by doing right in obedience to the divine will. Even the
psalms and Wisdom Literature are full of image. In Psalm 18:19,
David leaps over a wall by faith. In Proverbs 22:13 and 26:13,
Solomon tells of the sluggard who refuses to go into the street
for fear of meeting a lion. The narratives of the four Gospels and
Acts make up well over half of the New Testament. Who could
deny that the Book of Revelation is filled with vibrant imagery,
as is the majority of other prophetic writings?

If you took the concrete images and applicational cases out of
the epistles you would have looted these great letters of their
vibrancy and force. Paul and James constantly use Old Testament
examples to explain, compare, contrast, and seal their arguments.
The writer of Hebrews fills his letter with Jesus Christ, angels,
Melchizedek, king of Salem, and a vivid parade of other saints.
In chapter 12 he drives home his major point by asserting that
if we fail to live by faith we may become like profane Esau. The
preaching of Jesus leaps into life with the vitality of his images.
Take these images out of the Sermon on the Mount and it would
be a dry skeleton.

The gospel of our Lord Jesus Christ is a concrete example of
an emotion-producing event. That specific event in history
changed the course of human destiny. I have often wondered if
the Catholic fathers chose to leave Christ on the cross of the cru-
cifix because of its powerful emotional impact. I prefer the image
of the risen Lord and the empty tomb. My point is simple. Without these images Christianity is uncommunicable.

Sources of Illustrations

Illustrations are everywhere. For most of us the problem is getting them into a file that will allow us to access them when we need them. The 3 x 5 card file used to be state of the art. Today it is the electronic database. A flat bed scanner with OCR (optical character recognition) software that permits editing of the text is essential. Read avidly. Put a Post-it note on the page that you would like to retain with an indication of the topic that should go in the file. If you have access to professional assistance, have the page scanned, edited, and entered into your database. If you don't have professional help, train volunteers for this vital task. You will probably not get time to do this work yourself. Work smart and delegate. Get a system and keep adding regularly. Don't let it pile up.

There are two illustration books that set a standard for such material. First is Michael P. Green's *Illustrations for Biblical Preaching*. Green's book is an excellent example of how to write illustrations and assign topics. This book is also available in electronic form.[3] Craig Brian Larson's *Illustrations for Preaching & Teaching From Leadership Journal* provides an excellent example of editing illustrations.[4]

One of the most significant places for finding illustrations in our current world is the Internet. There are many sources there, and more are being added regularly. Learn to read newspapers and magazines on the Internet. This will allow you to download the article that interests you directly into your word processor. This makes a much easier transition to sermon or data base.

Happy hunting! Happier finding!

Supporting Rather Than Stealing

Now let's return to the title of this chapter. One of the problems I have noted in my own ministry and that of others is the lack of appropriate illustrations. When I ask other preachers about this, they say, "I couldn't find the right illustration so I didn't use one." I have even heard, "I know that illustration didn't really work but it was all I could find."

Most of us know what needs to be clarified by illustration. Not to illustrate when we need to do so steals interest and makes the sermon boring. To use the wrong illustration because we couldn't find the right one steals clarity. The answer is to get organized. Collect and file illustrations. Think about trading illustration files with other preachers. Use the Internet. The sermon that Haddon Robinson would grade an "A" must be illustrated appropriately, supporting the big idea.

For Further Reflection

Getting the Idea

1. What is this chapter talking about?
2. What is this chapter saying about what it's talking about?

Building on the Idea

1. What are the primary elements of illustrating sermons?
2. What role should illustrations play in the communication and development of the idea?
3. When illustrating, why is it so important to place a picture in your listener's mind?

Recommended Reading

Chapell, Bryan. *Using Illustrations to Preach with Power.* Grand Rapids: Zondervan, 1992.
Deffner, Don. *The Real Word for the Real World: Applying the Word to the Needs of People.* St. Louis: Concordia, 1977.

Flynn, Leslie B. *Come Alive with Sermon Illustrations: How to Find, Use and File Good Stories for Sermons and Speeches.* Grand Rapids: Baker, 1987.

Grant, Reg and John Reed. *Telling Stories to Touch the Heart.* Wheaton, IL: Victor Books, 1990.

Hostetler, Michael J. *Illustrating the Sermon.* Grand Rapids: Zondervan, 1989.

Louis Paul Lehman, *How to Find and Develop Effective Illustrations* (Grand Rapids: Kregel, 1985).

McQuilkin, J. Robinson. *Understanding and Applying the Bible.* Rev. ed. Chicago: Moody, 1992.

Toulmin, Stephen, Richard Rieke, and Allan Janik. *An Introduction to Reasoning.* New York: MacMillan, 1979.

Philosophy versus Method

Big Idea Preaching's Adaptability

Scott M. Gibson

Expository preaching is the communication of a biblical concept, derived from and transmitted through a historical, grammatical, and literary study of a passage in its context, which the Holy Spirit first applies to the personality and experience of the preacher, then through him/her to his/her hearers.[1]

This book is about preaching—good, clear, biblical preaching. All the authors in this volume consider it important that the explanation, interpretation, or application of a single dominant idea is drawn from one passage or several passages of Scripture. This is "big idea" preaching.

From reading the preceding chapters one discovers the versatility and adaptability of a single idea-oriented sermon. The idea, as the above definition from Haddon Robinson asserts, is the transmission of a biblical concept to one's listeners. This idea is understood from careful study tested in thoughtful personal reflection and application and then applied further to a particular audience.

Like the definition, this book began with a discussion of a philosophical foundation. Big idea preaching is built on a long-accepted strategy of rhetorical theory and practice combined with a solid evangelical hermeneutic. The result is clarity. The single idea of the text is communicated to listeners whom the preacher understands. The idea is brought from the ancient world to the modern world through the preacher's perception, appreciation, and understanding of the audience. Effective preaching is like this—it is clear and it connects.

But there are issues with which the big idea preacher must deal. This is marked out in the remainder of the book. One challenge is found in the Bible's use of genres. The Old and New Testaments employ various genres that raise questions about the task of searching out the idea. Likewise, the preacher faces a possibly equal challenge—exegeting one's culture. The responsible exegete understands his or her Bible and his or her culture. This is a biblical and theological reality, for the truth strikes men and women intellectually and emotionally. As preachers our goal is to hit the head and the heart.

Another way the preacher connects with listeners is by capturing the biblical author's flow of thought. When a preacher wrestles with the text and appreciates the biblical author's progression of ideas, and then comes to an understanding of the listeners' questions, the preacher can determine the flow of a sermon. A clear idea with a clear flow will allow listeners to grasp it and respond appropriately.

The response means transformation. Transformation takes place when the preacher bridges the text to the listener in ways that will allow the listener to understand the idea and experience change. All that has gone on prior to the communication of the idea—the study and audience analysis—now pours out through the personality and experience of the preacher's words and images. The idea is transferred to the minds and hearts of the listeners and they are changed.

We preach to change lives. A central idea sermon enables both preacher and listener to be clear about the change to which Scripture is calling him or her. This book is an attempt to help preachers become clear in their thinking and preaching so that they might help their listeners understand the Scripture and become the people God wants them to be.

Forming the One Idea

Haddon Robinson has taught us that formulating an idea comes as the result of finding the subject and the complement. The subject asks the question, "What is the author talking about?" The subject is best worded as a question—who, what, when, where, why, which, how. We can learn about the formation of an idea from one of Robinson's sermons from Genesis 3:1–6, "A Case Study in Temptation."[2] The text reads:

> Now the serpent was more crafty than any of the wild animals the Lord God had made. He said to the woman, "Did God really say, 'You must not eat from any tree in the garden'?"
>
> The woman said to the serpent, "We may eat fruit from the trees in the garden, but God did say, 'You must not eat fruit from the tree that is in the middle of the garden, and you must not touch it, or you will die.'"
>
> "You will not surely die," the serpent said to the woman. "for God knows that when you eat of it your eyes will be opened, and you will be like God, knowing good and evil."
>
> When the woman saw that the fruit of the tree was good for food and pleasing to the eye, and also desirable for gaining wisdom, she took some and ate it. She also gave some to her husband, who was with her, and he ate it.

Robinson's reply to the question, "What is the author talking about?" is answered by his subject:

Subject: How does Satan tempt us?

The complement completes the subject. It fills out the question by asking its own question: "What is the author saying about what he's talking about?" In this case Robinson determines that there is a double complement:

Complement: He comes to us in disguise
and he levels his attack against God.

Then, the subject and complement are combined and an idea is shaped. The interrogative is sliced off and an indicative statement is formed. This is the idea, sometimes called the exegetical idea. The idea is phrased in the following manner:

Subject + Complement = Idea
Idea: Satan tempts us when he comes to us in disguise
and he levels his attack against God.

After formulating the exegetical idea, a homiletical idea is created. The homiletical idea is a pithy restatement of the exegetical idea. It remains faithful to the intention of the text by capturing the idea in a way in which listeners will understand. Robinson phrases his homiletical idea this way:

Homiletical Idea: Satan comes to us in disguise to cause us to
distrust God's character and to doubt God's Word.

Finally, the preacher determines the purpose of the sermon. The purpose corresponds to the purpose of the passage and is worded for results. "As a result of hearing this sermon, I want my listeners to. . . ." The preacher fills in the blank with something that he wants the listener to know, an insight to be gained, an attitude to be developed, or a skill to be honed. For this sermon, Robinson develops the purpose:

Purpose: As a result of hearing this sermon, I want to help my
listeners to guard against the tempter by knowing his
strategy of attack.

The "big idea" preaching method is not stilted but lithe. Robinson gives us a method that is flexible. It is not a cookie-cutter-manufactured approach to preaching. It is philosophically and theologically solid, yet practical. Big idea preaching contains adaptability in its encounter with biblical genres; in the way sermons are shaped; and in light of one's audience and occasion.

Adaptability with Biblical Genres

Whether the genre is history, letter, narrative, poetry or prophecy, the method remains the same: What is the author talking about? What is the author saying about what he's talking about? Certainly the preacher needs to be aware of the nuances of the genres. As Bruce Waltke advises in chapter 3, literary source criticism and form criticism issues may influence the way in which a passage is understood; otherwise one may be left with fragments or, worse, eisegetical sermons.

Through careful work, the preacher can determine the idea of a passage. "As he studies," says Robinson, "the preacher wrestles with exegesis and hermeneutics—materials of grammar, history, literary forms, the thought and cultural settings of his text."[3] Sadly, he notes, "Every Sunday ministers claiming a high regard for the Scriptures preach on texts whose ideas they either do not understand or have not bothered to study."[4]

As an example of the preacher's need to study and understand genre and context, Robinson suggests a passage to consider. He observes that there are scores of sermons on prayer that have been based on the wording of Matthew 18:19, 20: "Again I say to you, that if two of you agree on earth about anything that they may ask, it shall be done for them by My Father who is in heaven. For where two or three have gathered together in My name, there am I in the midst." He writes:

> At first glance, Jesus endorses prayer offered in groups of two or three and promises that if Christians agree together about a prayer request somehow they bind the Father in heaven. Good sense, if nothing else, would drive us to scrutinize the context of those verses (If two or three Christian Dallas Cowboy fans agree to ask God for victory in an upcoming game and if a few Christians on

the opposing team pray for a Cowboy defeat, which group is God bound to answer?).

Actually, Jesus' Words here have little to do with the subject of prayer but instead with how sinning Christians should be restored. In the immediate context, the "two or three" does not refer to a small group prayer meeting but to the witnesses summoned in verse 16. "But if he (the sinning brother) does not listen to you, take one or two more with you, so that by the mouth of two or three witnesses every fact may be confirmed." All that Jesus says, therefore, applies to Christians dealing with someone who has sinned. The old maxim reminds us that "a text without its context becomes a pretext." In battling for the inspiration of individual words of Scripture we sometimes forget that words are merely "semantic markers for a field of meaning." Particular statements must be understood within the broader thought of which they are a part or what we teach may not be God's Word at all.[5]

Careful study is important. Appreciation of genre and context is key to responsible preaching. But study in the genres and backgrounds takes work. What we find is that no matter what genre we wade through, we can discover the idea. And it is this idea that serves as the constant in communicating the clear meaning of the text. The next step is communicating the idea. We will see that the shape of the communication of the one idea can also be varied.

Adaptability with Sermon Shapes

Sermon form is debatable. Content is not. The shape of the sermon varies. The idea remains the same. Yet for too long the shape of sermons has been standardized, consisting of three points, reflecting Greco-Roman rhetoric. Sermons like these often ignore the form of the passage—to the sermon's detriment. In cases like this, appreciation of the genre of a passage means nothing when one comes to shaping the sermon. Preachers who ignore the genre and context habitually shape their sermons the same way, ignoring the flow of the passage. But this does not have to be the case. Sermon form is flexible, depending on the type of passage and its flow, its purpose, and its audience. Robinson writes:

> Biblical preaching should not only be true to the Bible in its central ideas but in the development of those ideas as well. Many sermons that begin in the Bible stray from it in their structures. Homiletical methods sometimes tempt the minister to impose an arrangement of thought on a text foreign to that of the inspired writer. To be truly biblical, the major assertions supporting the sermon's basic concept must also be taken from the passage on which it is based.[6]

As Fred Craddock observes, "Even though that rhetoric [Greco-Roman] dominated the field of homiletics for centuries, not even that pattern for oral presentations can justifiably be called *the* form of a sermon. It remains the case to this day that a sermon is defined more by content and purpose than by form."[7] The sermon form is integrally part of the sermon, driving the idea home to the listener. The beauty of big idea preaching is that no matter what shape the sermon takes, the idea remains the same. This gives freedom to the preacher. In light of this, Craddock says, "The form of . . . a sermon is therefore a part of the warp and woof of the message itself and was not laid as a grid over the message, alien to it and rising from another source."[8]

"To be truly biblical," writes Robinson, "the major assertions supporting the sermon's basic concept must also be taken from the passage on which it is based." A preacher may rearrange material along psychological lines, but "whatever the outline the sermon assumes—and this can vary with the audience, speaker, or occasion—its content should reflect the argument of the biblical author and ought at every place be controlled by the writer's thought."[9] The central idea sermon is rooted in the text and is shaped by the author's thought, sensitive to the genre. Otherwise the preacher is in danger of missing the point of the passage, either veering his listeners into biblical misapplication or having them settle for platitudes.

The sermon can take on many shapes—deductive, inductive, or a little of both. As in the case of some of the parables, the passage may be shaped inductively. The preacher may choose to form the sermon inductively to reflect the author's thought, thereby keeping tension. This is especially the case when the audience may be familiar with a given text. Induction is perhaps the best way to reach them since they heard it before—again and again. Craddock calls preaching this way "overhearing" what the text has to say.[10]

Narrative preaching as a sermon form can provide a creative way to present the big idea, to hear it in a different way. One of my students presented a narrative about Mary as found in Luke 1. She spoke in the first person, as if she were Mary, telling her story and, toward the end, she gave us the homiletical idea: God chooses the ordinary to do extraordinary things. The form was narrative/inductive but the single idea came through clearly. And since the genre itself is narrative, the sermon was a success.

Preaching is tough work. It requires study and careful analysis of the text and its context. A central idea sermon adapts to the various genres of the Bible and finds flexibility in the way it is shaped. Sermon form helps communicate the intention of the text. However, one of the strongest influences on sermon form is the audience.

Adaptability to One's Audience

Big idea preaching provides a focus. The idea of the passage gives clarity for the preacher and the listener. Not only this, but we discover that the biblical author wrote with a purpose. "A sermon constructed out of honest exegesis and sound hermeneutics will also be true to the Bible in its purpose, the purpose describes what the truth is intended to accomplish."[11] The biblical writer had a specific audience in mind. The challenge to preachers is to understand the purpose of the author and then determine the purpose of the sermon for their listeners. Once this is established, the sermon can be formed.

The focus of the single idea sermon allows the preacher to ask how the text might be applied to specific listeners. How does this idea strike those who hear it? Robinson writes, "Truth is never more powerfully experienced than when it speaks to someone's personal situation."[12] One way to get at this is to imagine that you have three to five people from your congregation seated around your desk as you prepare the sermon. Think about the questions that each person might ask about a given text. With people like that looking over your shoulder, you will soon be pushed from generalities to particulars. You will focus on applying the one idea.

Not only does big idea preaching help with application; it also is sensitive to audience comprehension. Numerous lists, complicated points, and subpoints can fog in one's listeners with overwhelming details. Big idea preaching is not simplistic. It is clear. Children will understand. Teens will grasp the idea. Adults will thank you for your clarity.

What we discover is that big idea preaching has the potential to adjust to the audience and occasion with singular clarity. It helps the preacher understand his or her listeners and allows for clear application and connection with listeners because it is understandable.

Conclusion

This book is about preaching—good, clear, biblical preaching. The method of discovering one idea from the text can be used with the various biblical genres. Big idea preaching allows for the flexibility of sermon forms, and is sensitive to the needs of the audience. This method is what good, clear, biblical preaching is about.

Haddon Robinson has labored to make the message of the Bible clear to his own listeners and through those whom he has taught. The central idea sermon does just that—it gives the listener the big idea of the text in a clear way. Once the listener understands the Bible, his or her life will never be the same. And to God's glory that is what preaching is all about.

For Further Reflection

Getting the Idea

1. What is this chapter talking about?
2. What is this chapter saying about what it's talking about?

Building on the Idea

1. What are the important features of "big idea" preaching?
2. What are the challenges you face as you attempt to use the central idea approach to preaching?
3. With what sermon forms are you most comfortable? Why? How can you stretch yourself in experimenting with other sermon forms?

Recommended Reading

Craddock, Fred B. *Overhearing the Gospel: Preaching and Teaching the Faith to Persons Who Have Heard It all Before.* Nashville: Abingdon, 1978.

Robinson, Haddon W. *Biblical Preaching.* Grand Rapids: Baker, 1980.

———. "Homiletics and Hermeneutics." In *Hermeneutics, Inerrancy and the Bible,* ed. Earl D. Radmacher and Robert D. Preus. Grand Rapids: Zondervan/Acadamie, 1984.

———. "Preaching to Everyone in Particular: How to Scratch Where People Niche." *Leadership* 15, no. 4 (fall 1994): pp. 99–103.

———. "What is Expository Preaching?" In *Bibliotheca Sacra* 131: 521 (January 1974): pp. 55–60.

Notes

Introduction

1. Leslie R. Keylock, "Evangelical Leaders You Should Know: Meet Haddon W. Robinson," *Moody,* December 1986, 71–72. This introduction closely follows Keylock's article.

2. Quoted in ibid., 72.

3. Ibid.

Chapter 1. A Bullet versus Buckshot

1. Haddon W. Robinson, *Biblical Preaching: The Development and Delivery of Expository Messages* (Grand Rapids: Baker, 1980), 33.

2. Cf. Raymond Bailey, ed., *Hermeneutics for Preaching: Approaches to Contemporary Interpretations of Scripture.* (Nashville: Broadman, 1992); D. A. Carson, *Biblical Interpretation and the Church: The Problem of Contextualization* (Nashville: Thomas Nelson, 1984); Elliott E. Johnson, *Expository Hermeneutics: An Introduction* (Grand Rapids: Zondervan, 1990); William W. Klein, Craig L. Blomberg, and Robert L. Hubbard, *Introduction to Biblical Interpretation* (Dallas: Word, 1993); and Grant R. Osborne, *The Hermeneutical Spiral: A Comprehensive Introduction to Biblical Interpretation* (Downers Grove: InterVarsity, 1991).

3. Gordon D. Fee and Douglas Stuart, *How to Read the Bible for All Its Worth* (Grand Rapids: Zondervan, 1993), 16–17.

4. Kenneth S. Kantzer and Carl F. H. Henry, *Evangelical Affirmations* (Grand Rapids: Zondervan, 1990), 32.

5. Grant R. Osborne, *The Hermeneutical Spiral: A Comprehensive Introduction to Biblical Interpretation* (Downers Grove: InterVarsity, 1991), 8.

6. Paul Feinberg, "The Meaning of Inerrancy," in *Inerrancy,* ed. Norman Geisler (Grand Rapids: Zondervan, 1979), 267–304.

7. Paul J. Achtemeier, *The Inspiration of Scripture: Problems and Proposals* (Philadelphia: Westminster, 1980).

8. David Wells, "Word and World: Biblical Authority and the Quandary of Modernity," in *Evangelical Affirmations,* ed. Kenneth S. Kantzer and Carl F. H. Henry (Grand Rapids: Zondervan, 1990), 153–75.

9. Robinson, *Biblical Preaching,* 33.

10. Walter L. Liefeld, *New Testament Exposition: From Text to Sermon* (Grand Rapids: Zondervan, 1984), 5.

11. Robinson, *Biblical Preaching,* 39–44.

12. See Elliott E. Johnson, *Expository Hermeneutics: An Introduction* (Grand Rapids: Zondervan, 1990); Walter C. Kaiser Jr., *Toward an Exegetical Theology* (Grand Rapids: Baker, 1981); and William W. Klein, Craig L. Blomberg, and

Robert L. Hubbard, *Introduction to Biblical Interpretation* (Dallas: Word, 1993).

13. Timothy S. Warren, "A Paradigm for Preaching," *Bibliotheca Sacra* 148 (October–December 1991): 463–86.

14. Timothy S. Warren, Periodical Review of "The Crisis in Expository Preaching Today," in *Preaching* 11, no. 2 (September–October 1995): 4–12; *Bibliotheca Sacra* (April–June 1996): 230–31.

15. The applicational meaning communicated in the sermon will not be identical to the meaning intended for the original readers, but it must be clear that the application (that which is truly homiletical) emerges from the meaning intended for the original readers. See Warren, "A Paradigm."

16. 2 Timothy 3:16a, NIV.

17. The "big idea" is Robinson's term for the "bullet" or central proposition or thesis of the entire sermon. See Robinson, *Biblical Preaching*, 31–48.

18. Duane Litfin, *Public Speaking: A Handbook for Christians*, 2nd ed. (Grand Rapids: Baker, 1992), 80.

19. 358^a–1359^b.

20. A good case for the value of a single proposition can be found in Litfin, *Public Speaking*, 80–83. A less direct case is stated in Bryan Chapell, *Christ-centered Preaching: Reclaiming the Expository Sermon* (Grand Rapids: Baker, 1994). 139–42. A more subtle line of the same argument appears in the popular speech-helps book, William T. Brooks, *High Impact Public Speaking* (Englewood Cliffs, N.J.: Prentice Hall, 1988), 105–6.

21. Litfin, *Public Speaking*, 80–83. See John Cerella, John Rybash, William Hoyer, and Michael L. Camera, eds., *Adult Information Processing: Limits on Loss* (New York: Academic, 1993).

22. Nilsson, *The Point* (Chicago: Dunbar Music, 1970).

23. Richard E. Crable, *Argumentation as Communication: Reasoning with Receivers* (Columbus, Ohio: Charles E. Merill, 1976), 1–20.

24. Litfin, *Public Speaking*, 81.

25. Stephen Toulmin, Richard Rieke, and Allan Janik, *Introduction to Reasoning* (New York: Macmillan, 1979), 45–52.

26. See I. A. Richards, *The Philosophy of Rhetoric* (New York: Oxford University Press, 1965).

Chapter 2. Biblical Preaching That Adapts and Contexualizes

1. Calvin Miller, *Spirit, Word, and Story* (Dallas: Word, 1989), 102.

2. Haddon Robinson, *Biblical Preaching: The Development and Delivery of Expository Messages* (Grand Rapids: Baker, 1980), 27–28.

3. Haddon Robinson, *Biblical Sermons* (Grand Rapids: Baker, 1989), 10.

4. Ibid.

5. Thomas Oden, *Pastoral Theology: Essentials of Ministry* (San Francisco: Harper & Row, 1983), 132.

6. *The Homilies of St. John Chrysostom on the Statutes*, trans. Members of the English Church, Library of Fathers, vol. 9 (Oxford: John Henry Parker, 1842), 51–53, reprinted in *20 Centuries of Great Preaching*, ed. Clyde Fant and William Pinson, vol. 1 (Waco: Word, 1971), 79.

7. Ibid., 80

8. Ibid.

9. Ibid., 86 (rephrased from the "Old English" into contemporary terminology).

10. Ibid., 85.

11. *The Homilies of St. John on the Statutes*, quoted by Robert Payne, "Preaching to Dread and Panic," in *Christian History*, vol. 13, no. 4, 15.

12. Quoted by Warren Thomas Smith, *Augustine: His Life and Thought* (Atlanta: John Knox, 1980), 121–22.

13. William Bright, *Lessons from the Lives of Three Great Fathers* (London: Longmans, Green, 1890), 133.

14. Malcolm Muggeridge, *A Third Testament* (Boston: Little, Brown, 1976), 47.

15. Quoted in ibid., 47–48.

16. Quoted in Hugh Pope, *St. Augustine of Hippo* (New York: Image, 1961), 168.

17. Quoted in Muggeridge, *A Third Testament*, 47.

18. Quoted in Pope, *St. Augustine of Hippo*, 165.

19. Quoted in ibid., 176.

20. Quoted in Miller, *Spirit, Word, and Story*, 198.

21. Quoted in *Christian History*, vol. 12, no. 3, 2.

22. Ibid.

23. Ewald M. Plass, ed., *What Luther Says* (St. Louis: Concordia, 1959), 1130.

24. *Luther's Works: Sermons,* ed. and trans. John W. Doberstein, vol. 1 (Philadelphia: Muhlenberg, 1959), 72.

25. Plass, *What Luther Says*, 1130.

26. *Luther's Works: Sermons*, vol. 1, 151.

27. Ibid.

28. Plass, *What Luther Says*, 1129.

29. *Luther's Works: Sermons*, vol. 1, 72.

30. Ibid., xix.

31. Martin Luther King Jr., *Stride Toward Freedom: The Montgomery Story* (New York: Harper & Row, 1958), 63, quoted in Fant and Pinson, *20 Centuries of Great Preaching*, vol. 12, 356.

32. Martin Luther King Jr., "The Man Who Was a Fool," quoted in Fant and Pinson, *20 Centuries of Great Preaching*, vol. 12, 382–83.

33. Martin Luther King Jr., "Answer to a Perplexing Question," quoted in Fant and Pinson, *20 Centuries of Great Preaching*, vol. 12, 369.

34. Ibid., 371.

35. Ibid., 370.

36. Martin Luther King Jr., "I Have a Dream," reprinted in Lenwood G. Davis, *I Have a Dream . . . The Life and Times of Dr. Martin Luther King Jr.* (Westport, Conn.: Negro University Press, 1969), 263.

37. Ibid.

Chapter 3. Old Testament Interpreation Issues for Big Idea Preaching

1. Robert Polzin, *Samuel and the Deuteronomist: A Literary Study of the Deuternomic History,* pt. 2, *1 Samuel* (San Francisco:: Harper & Row, 1989).

2. Foundational works include Robert Alter, *The Art of Biblical Narrative* (New York: Basic Books, 1981); Robert Alter and Frank Kermode, eds., *The Literary Guide to the Bible* (Cambridge, Mass.: Belknap, 1987); Shimon Bar-Efrat, *Narrative Art in the Bible*, JSOT Supplements Series 70; Bible and Literature Series, no. 17 (Sheffield, England: Almond, 1989); Adele Berlin, *Poetics and Interpretation of Biblical Narrative*, JSOT, Supplements Series; Bible and Literature Series, no. 9 (Sheffield, England: Almond, 1983); Tremper Longman III, *Literary Approaches to Biblical Interpretation* (Grand Rapids: Zondervan, 1987); Richard L. Pratt Jr., *He Gave Us Stories* (Brentwood, Tenn.: Wohlegmuth & Hyatt, 1990); Mark Allan Powell, *What Is Narrative Criticism?* (Minneapolis: Fortress, 1990); Jean Louis Ska, *"Our Fathers Have Told Us": Introduction to the Analysis of Hebrew Narratives* (Roma: Editrice Pontificio Istituto Biblico, 1990); Meir Sternberg, *The Poetics of Biblical Narrative: Ideological Literature and the Drama of Reading*, The Indiana Literary Biblical Series (Bloomington: Indiana University Press, 1985).

3. The repetition of the palatals /k~q~g/ that ripples through the unit in phonological harmony with *kesil* ("fool") also unifies the work. Verse 1 sets the stage: *kasseleg baqqayis wekammatar baqqaysir ken lo' na'weh lekesil kabod.* Apart from the prefixes, every word apart from "not fitting"(!), begins with /k~q/.

4. Arndt Meinhold, *Die Sprueche*, in *Zuercher Bibelcommentare* 16.2 (Zurich: Theologischer Verlag, 1991), 436.

5. Haddon W. Robinson, *Biblical Preaching: The Development and Delivery of Expository Messages* (Grand Rapids: Baker, 1980), 39f.

6. Cf. Raymond C. Van Leeuwen, *Context and Meaning in Proverbs 25–27* (Atlanta: Scholars, 1988), 88f.

7. Van Leeuwen (100) says "the idea of fittingness is the poem's central concern." Although we all stand in debt to Van Leeuwen's brilliant dissertation, "fittingness" is an inadequate summarization.

8. The English versions obscure the unique syntax of *k + k + ken* "like [snow/a fluttering sparrow] . . . like [rain/darting swallow]. so [honor/an undeserved curse . . .]."

9. "Sparrow" and "swallow" are glosses; the precise genre or species of birds is uncertain.

10. The images are so creative and absurd they confound pedestrian and prosaic commentators, who want to tame them. Even the NIV alters the normal meaning of verse 9A, "a thorn bush grows up in the hand of the drunkard," to "a thorn bush in the hand of a drunkard." Delitzsch defended the meaning of the NIV from Mishnaic Hebrew, not from biblical Hebrew, and my own research calls into question his lexicography.

11. Duane A. Garrett, *Proverbs, Ecclesiastes, Song of Songs*, The New American Commentary 14 (Nashville: Broadman, 1993), 212.

12. The image of a thorn bush growing up in the drunkard's hand is an incomplete metaphor. A thorn bush does not grow in any hand. However, the image forces one to realize that as it took time for the vegetation to grow up there, so also it took time for the fool to memorize the proverbs. How else did they get in his mouth?

13. Meinhold, *Die Sprueche*, 439.

14. Garrett, *Proverbs, Ecclesiastes, Song of Songs*, 212.

15. A drunkard in the Old Testament is no down-and-out bum. Many of its thirteen references to drunkenness explicitly or inferentially refer to kings (1 Kings 16:9; 20:16; Isa. 28:1, 3) and the wealthy (1 Sam. 25:36), who could afford the quantities required.

16. So W. Gunther Plaut, *Book of Proverbs*, The Jewish Commentary for Bible Readers (New York: Union of American Hebrew Congregations, 1961), 268.

17. So Raymond C. Van Leeuwen, *The Book of Proverbs*, The New Interpreter's Bible, vol. 5 (Nashville: Abingdon, 1997). 225.

18. So Meinhold, *Die Sprueche*, 440.

Chapter 6. Preaching the Big Idea to Cultures and Subcultures

1. Haddon W. Robinson, *Biblical Preaching: The Development and Delivery of Expository Messages* (Grand Rapids: Baker, 1980), 77–78.

2. Ibid., 78–79.

3. Neil Postman, *Amusing Ourselves to Death: Public Discourse in the Age of Show Business* (New York: Penguin, 1985), 79.

4. From a Haddon Robinson sermon at Denver Seminary on January 4, 1991, focusing on mass media, seminary education, and the church. All other subsequent Robinson quotes in this chapter are from this same address, unless indicated otherwise.

5. Luigi and Allesandra Manca, "The Siren's Song: A Theory of Subliminal Seduction," published in *Mediamerica, Mediaworld*, 5th ed. (Belmont, Calif.: Wadsworth, 1993), 298–300.

6. Ned B. Stonehouse, "The Areopagus Address," in *Paul Before the Areopagus and Other New Testament Studies* (Grand Rapids: Eerdmans, 1957), 1–40, quoted in *Biblical Preaching*, 85.

7. The remainder of this chapter is based on material in Terry Mattingly's annual "And Now a Word from Your Cul-

ture" lectures, given in the Doctor of Ministry in preaching program at Gordon-Conwell Theological Seminary. See also the chapter with the same title in *Shaping Our Future: Challenges for the Church in the Twenty-First Century* (Cambridge and Boston: Cowley, 1994), 130–44.

8. John Fischer, *What On Earth Are We Doing? Finding Our Place as Christians in the World* (Ann Arbor, Mich.: Servant, 1996), 119.

Chapter 7. The Big Idea and Biblical Theology's Grand Theme

1. Fred B. Craddock, *Preaching* (Nashville: Abingdon, 1985), 49.

2. Walter J. Burghardt, *Preaching: The Art and the Craft,* (New York: Paulist, 1987), 34.

3. Eugene Peterson, *Answering God* (San Francisco: HarperCollins, 1989), 11.

4. Phillips Brooks, *Lectures on Preaching* (London: Griffith, Farran, Okeden & Welsh, 1886), 126.

5. John 3:21 and John 14:6.

6. Ian Pitt-Watson, *A Primer for Preachers* (Grand Rapids: Baker, 1986), 99.

7. Brooks, *Lectures*, 17.

8. Ibid., 129.

9. Pitt-Watson, *Primer*, 102–3.

10. Burghardt, *Preaching*, 20.

11. Kenneth L. Woodward, "Heard Any Good Sermons Lately?" *Newsweek*, March 4, 1996, 50–52.

Chapter 10. Visualizing the Big Idea

1. Gordon W. Allport, "Eidetic Imagery," *British Journal of Psychology* 15 (October 1924): 99–120; Cynthia R. Gray and Kent Gummerman, "The Enigmatic Eidetic Image: A Critical Examination of Methods, Data, and Theories," *Psychological Bulletin* 82, no. 3 (1975): 383–407.

2. John W. Reed, ed., *1100 Illustrations from the Writings of D. L. Moody* (Grand Rapids: Baker, 1996); idem, ed., *Moody's Bible Characters Come Alive* (Grand Rapids: Baker, 1997).

3. Michael P. Green, ed., *Illustrations for Biblical Preaching,* (Grand Rapids: Baker, 1982).

4. Craig Brian Larsen, *Illustrations for Preaching and Teaching From Leadership Journal* (Grand Rapids: Baker, 1993).

Chapter 11. Philosophy versus Method

1. Haddon W. Robinson, *Biblical Preaching: The Development and Delivery of Expository Messages* (Grand Rapids: Baker, 1980), 30.

2. Haddon W. Robinson, ed., *Biblical Sermons* (Grand Rapids: Baker, 1989), 11–30.

3. Haddon W. Robinson, "Homiletics and Hermeneutics," in *Hermeneutics, Inerrancy and the Bible*, ed. Earl D. Radmacher and Robert D. Preus (Grand Rapids: Zondervan/Acadamie, 1984), 804.

4. Ibid., 805.

5. Ibid.

6. Ibid., 807.

7. Fred B. Craddock, *Preaching* (Nashville: Abingdon, 1985) 170.

8. Ibid., 189.

9. Robinson, "Homiletics and Hermeneutics," 807.

10. Fred B. Craddock, *Overhearing the Gospel: Preaching and Teaching the Faith to Persons Who Have Heard It All Before* (Nashville: Abingdon, 1978).

11. Robinson, "Homiletics and Hermeneutics," 808.

12. Haddon W. Robinson, "Preaching to Everyone in Particular: How to Scratch Where People Niche," *Leadership* 15, no. 4 (Fall 1994): 100.

Contributors

Paul Borden is a Church Growth Consultant for the American Baptist Churches of the West. Previously, he served as Executive Director of Teaching Church Network and Director Of Church Consulting for the Evangelical Free Church of America. Dr. Borden also served as Director of the Doctor of Ministry Program, Associate Professor of Homiletics, Academic Dean and Executive Vice President of Denver Seminary. He earned the Master of Theology (Th.M.) degree from Dallas Theological Seminary and the Doctor of Philosophy (Ph.D.) degree in Higher Education Administration from the University of Denver. Dr. Borden has over fifteen years of pastoral experience.

Scott M. Gibson is Assistant Dean and Assistant Professor of Ministry at Gordon-Conwell Theological Seminary, South Hamilton, MA, where he teaches homiletics. He earned the Master of Divinity (M.Div.) degree from Gordon-Conwell, the Master of Theology (Th.M.) degree in homiletics from Princeton Theological Seminary, the Master of Theology (M.Th.) degree in Church History from the University of Toronto and the Doctor of Philosophy (D.Phil.) degree in church history from the University of Oxford.

Duane Litfin is President of Wheaton College (Illinois). Dr. Litfin taught preaching for ten years at Dallas Theological Seminary and he has pastored churches in Indiana and Tennessee. He earned the Master of Theology degree from Dallas Theological Seminary, the Doctor of Philosophy (Ph.D.) degree in commu-

179

nication from Purdue University and the Doctor of Philosophy (D.Phil.) degree in New Testament studies from the University of Oxford.

Terry Mattingly teaches journalism at Milligan College (Tennessee) and is a popular syndicated columnist. He earned the Master of Science (M.S.) degree in journalism from the University of Illinois. He has done extensive work on the study of culture and its impact in the media.

John W. Reed is Senior Professor Emeritus of Pastoral Ministries at Dallas Theological Seminary, where he has taught preaching for over two decades. He earned the Master of Divinity (M.Div.) degree from Grace Theological Seminary (Indiana) and the Doctor of Philosophy (Ph.D.) degree in communication from the Ohio State University.

Bruce L. Shelley has taught church history and historical theology for forty years at Denver Seminary. He has authored or edited over twenty books. He earned the Master of Divinity (M.Div.) degree from Fuller Theological Seminary and the Doctor of Philosophy (Ph.D.) degree from the University of Iowa.

Joseph M. Stowell, III is president of Moody Bible Institute, Chicago. Dr. Stowell came to Moody after many years of pastoral ministry in Ohio, Indiana and Michigan. He earned the Master of Theology (Th.M.) degree from Dallas Theological Seminary. He was honored with a Doctor of Divinity (D.D.) degree from The Master's College (California) in 1987. He has written five books.

Donald R. Sunukjian teaches homiletics at Talbot School of Theology, California. He has many years of pastoral experience and also taught preaching at Dallas Theological Seminary. He earned the Master of Theology (Th.M.) and Doctor of Theology (Th.D.) degrees from Dallas Theological Seminary and the Doctor of Philosophy (Ph.D.) degree in communication from the University of California at Los Angeles.

Bruce Waltke is Professor of Old Testament Studies at Reformed Theological Seminary, Orlando FL, and Professor Emeritus at

Regent College, Vancouver, British Columbia. He earned the Doctor of Philosophy (Ph.D.) degree from Harvard University. He has written numerous scholar articles, served in pastoral ministry, and taught at nine schools of Theology.

Scott A. Wenig is Assistant Professor of Applied Theology at Denver Seminary and Associate Pastor of Centennial Community Church, Denver. Dr. Wenig teaches homiletics and church history. He earned the Master of Divinity (M.Div.) degree from Denver Seminary and the Doctor of Philosophy (Ph.D.) in history from the University of Colorado.

Keith Willhite is Associate Professor of Pastoral Ministries and Director of D.Min. Studies at Dallas Theological Seminary. He teaches communication and preaching. He has ten years of pastoral experience in churches in Texas, Indiana and Michigan. He earned the Master of Theology (Th.M.) degree from Dallas Theological Seminary and the Doctor of Philosophy (Ph.D.) degree in communication from Purdue University.